*The Good Shepherd,
Gentle Guide, and Gracious Host*

# The Good Shepherd, Gentle Guide, and Gracious Host

Metaphors and Meditations from the Twenty-Third Psalm

Patrick Allen

CASCADE *Books* • Eugene, Oregon

THE GOOD SHEPHERD, GENTLE GUIDE, AND GRACIOUS HOST
Metaphors and Meditations from the Twenty-Third Psalm

Copyright © 2020 Patrick Allen. All rights reserved. Except for brief quotations in critical publications or reviews, no part of this book may be reproduced in any manner without prior written permission from the publisher. Write: Permissions, Wipf and Stock Publishers, 199 W. 8th Ave., Suite 3, Eugene, OR 97401.

Cascade Books
An Imprint of Wipf and Stock Publishers
199 W. 8th Ave., Suite 3
Eugene, OR 97401

www.wipfandstock.com

PAPERBACK ISBN: 978-1-5326-7710-6
HARDCOVER ISBN: 978-1-5326-7711-3
EBOOK ISBN: 978-1-5326-7712-0

*Cataloguing-in-Publication data:*

Names: Allen, Patrick, author.
Title: The good shepherd, gentle guide, and gracious host : metaphors and meditations from the Twenty-Third Psalm / Patrick Allen.
Description: Eugene, OR: Cascade Books, 2020
Identifiers: ISBN 978-1-5326-7710-6 (paperback) | ISBN 978-1-5326-7711-3 (hardcover) | ISBN 978-1-5326-7712-0 (ebook)
Subjects: LCSH: Bible. Psalms, XXIII—Meditations.
Classification: BS1450 23D 2020 (print) | BS1450 (ebook)

Manufactured in the U.S.A.                                  MARCH 13, 2020

A Psalm of David (23) taken from The Holy Bible, Modern English Version MEV
Copyright 2014 by Military Bible Association.
Used by Permission. All rights reserved worldwide.

All other Scripture quotations unless otherwise noted are taken from The Holy Bible, New International Version NIV
Copyright 1973, 1978, 1984, 2011 by Biblica, Inc.
Used by Permission. All rights reserved worldwide.

This book is dedicated to my wife, Lori. She read every word of the manuscript, patiently listened to numerous versions of the ideas and stories contained herein, and offered wise counsel on how to organize the text and focus my thoughts for the benefit of the reader. She is my partner, my biggest cheerleader, and my pastor, too.

For me, it all comes down to this:
Life is messy, but God is faithful.

## Table of Contents

Preface ix
Introduction xiii

### PART I: THE GOOD SHEPHERD

Chapter 1:  The Lord is my shepherd—Protection  3
Chapter 2:  I shall not want—Plenty  17
Chapter 3:  He makes me lie down in green pastures—Rest  30
Chapter 4:  He leads me beside still waters—Serenity  41
Chapter 5:  He restores my soul—Renewal  55

### PART II: THE GENTLE GUIDE

Chapter 6:  He leads me in paths of righteousness
for his name's sake—Guidance  71
Chapter 7:  Even though I walk through the valley
of the shadow of death—Journey  84
Chapter 8:  I will fear no evil—Courage  98
Chapter 9:  For you are with me—Companionship  111
Chapter 10: Your rod and your staff,
they comfort me—Contentment  122

### PART III: THE GRACIOUS HOST

Chapter 11: You prepare a table before me
in the presence of my enemies—Provision  141
Chapter 12: You anoint my head with oil—Blessing  156
Chapter 13: My cup runs over—Overflow  168
Chapter 14: Surely goodness and mercy shall follow me
all the days of my life—Grace  181

Chapter 15: And I will dwell in the house of the Lord forever—Home  192

Closing Comments: The Good Shepherd, Gentle Guide, and Gracious Host  201

## *Preface*

I would not have written this book ten years ago. Honestly, I was too busy being busy—speaking in chapel, leading retreats, hiring faculty, writing reports, answering emails, attending one meeting after another, putting out fires, maintaining a campus presence, building my resume, worrying constantly, and trying to manage the stresses that come along with an administrative career in Christian higher education. While I deeply appreciated the sentiments of the Twenty-third Psalm, I didn't think I had the time for calm and careful reflection of any kind, let alone reflection on the Psalms, so I didn't make room for such activities. My work was just too important, I thought, for such extravagances, and sadly it crowded out many important elements that would have nurtured my spiritual growth.

Five years ago, I left administrative work and joined the university's teaching faculty. In essence, I traded money for time, and it is the best trade I have ever made. On more than one occasion, I came to the office with ample time to think and write, and thought, "They actually pay me for this. Wow! What a gift." Of course, I was expected to do more than just reflect and write, but I did have time for a lengthy, sustained writing project such as is required for a book. Without this gift of time, I would not have written this book.

And five years ago, I could not have written this book. Honestly, I didn't have a clue about how to set up a supportive work space and establish a disciplined writing schedule, or come up with a compelling idea, develop a book proposal, find a publisher, and write in keeping with a publisher's style manual. One afternoon in the fall of 2013, a departmental colleague walked up to me and asked if I was interested in writing a book together. I instantly said, "Yes!" although I didn't have a clue about what I was agreeing to do, and that started a writing partnership that resulted in two academic books. I learned so much about writing from these experiences. And in between the two co-authored books, I decided that I would write two devotional/spiritual discipline books based on prayers found in *Forward Day by Day*, a daily devotional reader published by Forward Movement, the publishing arm of the Episcopal Church. As a result, *Morning Resolve: To Live a Simple, Sincere, and Serene Life (2015)* and *For Today: A Prayer When Life Gets Messy (2018)* now see the light of day. Both books contained personal stories that struck a familiar chord with many readers, and that provided the encouragement I needed to think about another book using a similar format—stories, meditations, scriptural reflections, some practical advice, and questions for reflection and discussion. So, now I felt ready and able to write another book, but what should I write about this time around?

Honestly, I struggled to come up with an idea that would be life-giving to me, acceptable to my publisher, and helpful to a wider reading audience. I outlined five different book ideas, including an idea about metaphors and meditations on Psalm 23. When I shared this idea with my wife, Lori, she looked me squarely in the eyes and ask, "Are you sure the world needs another book on the Twenty-third Psalm?" I immediately agreed that I would go in another direction, but the other book ideas left me flat and floundering, while the idea of reflecting and writing on this particular psalm just kept nagging at me. Why?

Without doubt, the Twenty-third Psalm is my favorite psalm, and in fact, my favorite passage in the entire Bible. It is beautifully written and offers comfort and courage every time I read it. Surely, that is why it is read at so many funerals and memorial services, and in times of difficulty and trouble, too. It speaks to those who are suffering or wounded in one way or another, and that is all of us. To know that God will prepare a table before us in the presence of our enemies, right where we are in the midst of the battle, brings a steadfast confidence that we will never have to face our own tough and terrible times alone.

And it offers more than confidence. It offers grace and guidance and courage and hope—and more. It is a psalm as fitting for a celebration as for a funeral. Somehow it speaks to each of us in our darkest valleys and on our highest mountaintops, in our very best and worst moments, assuring us that whether it is our deepest fears and our highest hopes that arise from deep within us, God is present, offering grace, companionship, and courage. Given such a powerful message, in the end I had to write this book, one that invites reflection on Psalm 23 through the consideration of three metaphors—God as the good shepherd, the gentle guide, and the gracious host.

It is my hope that we, all of us, can learn the art of appropriation. That is, to read and reflect on the meditations I offer, and then draw from them and apply that which makes sense, that which encourages your spiritual walk as you make your way home. As such, this is not a book to provide a deeper understanding of formal theology or biblical exegesis. Honestly, I wouldn't be able to pull that off if I wanted to. I am not a trained theologian or an Old Testament scholar, but I am one who reads the Scriptures every day—carefully, prayerfully, and thoughtfully, and if my last two books are any evidence at all, I believe that my stories and devotional insights can provide us with something to chew on, to think about, to live out as we devote ourselves to loving God with everything we have and are, and loving our neighbors, too. If this book enriches your spiritual journey, then I have accomplished what I set out to do.

Of course, over the years there are countless individuals who have shaped my understanding of the Christian life and were kind enough to entertain some very fuzzy theological questions along the way, and a few silly ones, too. I can only name a few here—Rev. James Adams (my home church pastor in Saint Louis, Michigan), Dr. Randall Spindle (professor, Southern Nazarene University), Dr. Merle Strege (professor, Anderson University), and Dr. Michael Lodahl (professor, Point Loma Nazarene University). And my three fast friends, Dr. Ron Benefiel, Dr. Michael McKinney, and Dr. Dean Nelson (all professors at Point Loma Nazarene University), allowed me the privilege of examining not only my deepest questions and concerns, but gave room for my sheer doubts and fears, too. It is impossible to adequately explain how formative good friends can be, and they were—and still are.

I trust that this book will be formative for you, too. In one way or another, I believe that we are all on a spiritual journey or faith quest. May the metaphors and meditations that follow accompany and enrich your travels, and may we all come to see grace at work as we strive to love both God and neighbor as if our very lives depend on it. Honestly, I have come to believe that it does.

Patrick Allen
Newberg, Oregon
February 8, 2019

# *Introduction*

The metaphor is probably the most fertile power possessed by man.
—JOSÉ ORTEGA Y GASSETT

## Psalm 23

This book is a collection of fifteen meditations, organized around three metaphors from the Twenty-third Psalm, perhaps the most well-known and widely quoted passage in Holy Scripture, and certainly one of the most beloved passages found anywhere in the English language. In just six simple verses—about one hundred and twenty words, depending on the translation—we are transfixed by their message and deeply moved by their relevance to our lives. It is so powerful, so personal, seemingly written especially, perhaps solely, for each of us, regardless of how we found our way to this passage or the state of the world around us or in us. Why? What gives Psalm 23 such popularity, such possibility, such command? Why does it seem to connect so profoundly with the human spirit, with each of us, whether we are grieving, celebrating, hoping, or suffering—disappointed, disillusioned, afraid, alone, or on top of the world? The answer, I believe, has much to do with the approachable, inviting metaphors for God that are expressed in these six verses, and even more to do with the full gamut of human experience that emerges and the full range of human emotions that rise up within us when we read them—especially when they are read out loud, in community, in difficult, even desperate times. At one time or another, we have all been there, or we are there still.

Certainly, if we take a step back for a moment, we can see clearly that the psalms of David contain the full scope of human experience. In

Psalm 21, just two psalms before Psalm 23, we find the writer celebrating a time of thanksgiving:

**Psalm 21**

<sup>1</sup> How the king rejoices in your strength, O Lord!
He shouts with joy because you give him victory.
<sup>2</sup> For you have given him his heart's desire;
you have withheld nothing he requested.
<sup>3</sup> You welcomed him back with success and prosperity.
You placed a crown of finest gold on his head.
<sup>4</sup> He asked you to preserve his life,
and you granted his request.
The days of his life stretch on forever.
<sup>5</sup> Your victory brings him great honor,
and you have clothed him with splendor and majesty.

There is rejoicing with victory, success, prosperity, reward, splendor, majesty, and hope for a long life. What could be better than that! Yet in the first two verses of the very next psalm (22), we find these haunting words, some of which Jesus uttered as he suffered on the cross:

**Psalm 22**

<sup>1</sup> My God, my God, why have you forsaken me?
Why are you so far from saving me,
so far from my cries of anguish?
<sup>2</sup> My God, I cry out by day, but you do not answer,
by night, but I find no rest. (NIV)

We hear despair, alienation, fear, and discouragement in these words. Certainly, Jesus expressed them in the darkest moments of his life, and most of us have had those feelings way, too, whether we expressed them in words or simply carried them silently deep within our souls.

So, we find the full range of human experience, just about everything this life brings our way on the road between Psalm 21 to 22, and then we read Psalm 23, overflowing with experience, wisdom, hope, comfort, and gracious memories. I have come to believe that Psalm 23 was written by someone in old age, someone having journeyed the road from Psalm 21 to 22 and back again several times. It is, in many ways, an ultimate expression of faith in God who has been found to be a good shepherd, a gentle guide, and a gracious host. It is an acknowledgment that God is faithful, wise, gracious, dependable, and kind. This is a hard-won understanding, one that can only be gained, it seems to me, by living and experiencing all that life brings our way—the good, the bad, and the ugly. That is why the Twenty-third Psalm speaks to all of us, because we are on familiar territory somewhere on the journey between Psalm 21 and 22, carrying the hope of finding green pastures, still waters, and a table set before us, even if it is in the midst of our enemies. And we are far too often our own worst enemy.

You may be wondering—did King David write this psalm? Most scholars do not understand the reference to David in the superscription (*A psalm of David*) to refer to authorship in that way. True, this psalm has been traditionally associated with David. After all, he was at one time a shepherd himself, and he celebrated his share of victories and suffered a few humiliating defeats, too. Surely, he experienced enough of life to write such a beautiful tribute to God's constant presence and sustaining grace. However, it is not clear that David wrote it, or if someone else wrote it in a manner and style similar to David, or if someone wrote it in honor of David and dedicated it to him. As far as I am concerned, you can take your choice. Honestly, I do not really know or wish to debate the issue. It makes no difference at all for the purposes of this book. We will think together about the beauty and power of Psalm 23, and reflect on how the metaphors in Psalm 23 and the meditations that arise from them can further our appreciation of God's work in our individual lives and deepen our understanding of how God faithfully works among us, truly present, full of grace and truth.

Before we look a bit closer at the content and organization of the fifteen meditations in this book and how they are intended to be used, a few words about metaphors in general may be helpful. As we will see, the metaphors in Psalm 23 reveal something about the character of God, one who is good, gentle, and gracious—a God who is approachable and kind.

## Metaphors

What is a metaphor? Good question! Simply put, a metaphor is a description or comparison of something that helps you understand something else. It is a way to engender understanding of one kind of thing in terms of another, giving clarity, insight, and identity to that which is hidden, unclear, or mysterious. For example, if we say that Jill is a real tiger and Bobby is a shining star, you get a certain understanding of their behavior. Of course, Jill isn't really a tiger and Bobby isn't a member of the Milky

Way, but the metaphors give some insight into what to expect when they show up at your front door or volunteer at church. And if we say that your neighbor is just a big teddy bear or that his bark is worse than his bite (using a metaphor of a less-than-courageous watchdog), we gain some insight into your neighbor's temperament and get a picture of how he relates with you, at least on most occasions.

Of course, metaphors are never complete, and must be handled with care. They never provide the entire description or an all-encompassing understanding of a person or situation or phenomena. And confusion can arise when metaphors work at cross-purposes or provide different aspects of a person or event. Let me illustrate. What metaphor would you use to complete this sentence: A grandfather is a . . . ?

Some of us never knew our own grandfathers, so this question may have to be answered through a bit of speculation or observation of others' grandfathers. I had the privilege of knowing and spending summers with both of my grandfathers. One grandfather was simply fun to be with. He told good stories, teased each of his grandchildren in a kind and loving way, brought us treats and surprises, paid attention to all of us, loved sports, played games, and was always generous—and happy, too. The best metaphor I can come up with to describe him is that my grandfather was a big, kind, gentle teddy bear—easy to love. He did smoke a good deal and drink a beer or two on weekends. In my conservative religious family, that was a big no-no. And grandpa didn't go to church either—another concern for the family, but he was so loving and kind that we all wanted to be with him, and to be like him. We always sought out the company of the big teddy bear whenever we could.

My other grandfather was a devoutly religious man, a very hard worker, and a follower of all "the holiness rules." I'm sure he was deeply committed to his church and family, leading the family in devotions and prayer each morning, being sure that everyone knelt, paid attention, and took their turn praying out loud, but he came across as stern, joyless, critical, demanding, and demeaning to his grandchildren. The message we received was clear: if we were seen, we were not to be heard; and it would be better if we were not seen at all. He was a German Shepherd guard dog. All he had to do was stare in our direction and we would keep our distance. My brothers and I feared that if we became Christians, we would have to be mean and unpleasant. We didn't want that. Honestly, we preferred the company of the teddy bear—even if that put us in danger of eternal punishment.

So, it is easy for me to give you a metaphor for each of my grandfathers, although they were very different, but what happens when I try to provide a metaphor for a grandfather—not my grandfather but a grandfather? This is much more difficult because my own experiences with my two grandfathers leave me with two metaphors that are quite different, even contradictory.

The contrary and confusing nature of metaphors is important to keep in mind when we read Scripture. After all, the Bible is full of metaphors. In Matthew alone, there are at least a dozen descriptions of the kingdom. The kingdom is like a sower of seeds (13:24), a mustard seed (13:31), some yeast (13:33), a hidden treasure in a field (13:44), a merchant looking for a pearl of great price (13:45), a fishing net in the sea (13:47), an owner of a household (13:52), a king settling accounts with his servants (18:23), a landowner hiring workers (20:1), a king preparing a wedding banquet for his son (22:2), a wedding party waiting for the bridegroom (25:1), and a man going on a journey (25:14). As you can see, while each description gives us some insight and understanding into the nature of the kingdom of God, none of them portray the kingdom completely, and it is not easy to see the connection between a mustard seed, some yeast, a king, and a business traveler, or even what they have in common.

Jesus gave us seven "I am" statements, metaphors really, reported in the Gospel of John: I am the bread of life (6:35, 48, 51); I am the light of the world (8:12, 9:5); I am the gate of the sheep (10:7, 9); I am the good shepherd (10:11, 14); I am the resurrection and the life (11:25); I am the way, the truth, and the life (14:6); and I am the true vine (15:1). Jesus used these powerful metaphors to instruct his disciples and anyone else who would listen. They give us insight into the many-faceted nature of Jesus' ministry and purpose among us, for us, and in us. I think each of us can find meaning and connection with one or more of them. For me, the good shepherd and the true vine metaphors bring comfort and understanding. Still, I must confess that the connection between all the "I am" statements is not easy for me to see. I guess I am not all that good at connecting the dots.

In addition to the metaphors for the kingdom and Jesus' ministry, think of all the metaphors we have for God—some we glean from Scripture, some given to us by preachers, and others we just pick up along the way and carry around in our heads: king, sovereign, lord, creator, sustainer, avenging warrior, watchman, judge, rewarder, punisher, puppeteer, butler, parking attendant, wizard, fortress, rock, shelter, and friend, to name just a few. They all provide some insight into our understanding of God's identity and character. Most are helpful, but some of them lead to a conception of God as unkind, uncaring, judgmental, temperamental, even vindictive. And even magisterial metaphors such a lord, king, ruler, and sovereign are difficult for many Christians, and non-Christians, too, because these metaphors set God apart, literally placing God not only on a pedestal, but on a throne as well. Our job, it seems, is to enter the throne room and bow down, hoping to gain favor and receive a blessing. For me, this is not a helpful metaphor for a good, gentle, and gracious God. At the end of the day, conceptions and metaphors of a God as king and sovereign who deserves (and needs) our worship seem to me to be in tension with such metaphors as comforter, friend, and companion.

Let me be clear. I am not saying that magisterial metaphors are necessarily bad or inappropriate. They are not. Certainly, they are meaningful to many of us. In fact, magisterial metaphors are very likely the operative view of God for many Christians today, but I have to admit that such metaphors can limit the idea that God is approachable. This is one reason why Psalm 23 is so beloved. Here we find approachable metaphors: the good shepherd, the gentle guide, and the gracious host. These are metaphors that make God approachable, just as a grandfather teddy bear is more inviting than a grandfather German Shepherd.

The Bible contains over one hundred references to shepherds, and you don't find much mention of bad shepherds. Shepherds watch and protect their flocks, go after the lost lambs, and know each one by name. Likewise, there are many references to God as a guide, leading the Children of Israel out of Egypt, leading Joshua into the promised land, or leading John the Baptizer out to the wilderness beyond the Jordan River. Jesus himself promised that a comforter would be sent to us, the Spirit who would lead us into all truth. And stories of hosts providing a meal and rest to humans and angels alike run from Abraham to Joseph to Jesus, and continue throughout the New Testament. Without doubt, hospitality is a powerful spiritual practice, one of the true graces of the Christian faith.

These metaphors—shepherd, guide, and host—are caring and comforting understandings that invite us into God's presence. And the adjectives are just as heartening—good, gentle, and gracious. It is the combination of these nouns and adjectives and how they complement and affirm each other that make these metaphors so powerful, so beloved.

They bring elements of God's character and promise to the fore, insights hard won somewhere on the road between Psalm 21 and Psalm 22.

## Meditations

I want to end this introduction with a word or two about the meditations you will find in this book: what they are and what they are not, how the book is organized, and how I have envisioned these meditations to be used. To start, these meditations are not biblical exegesis, a term from the Greek meaning "to explain" or "to interpret," used since the early seventeenth century to refer to scriptural passages. I make no attempt to explore the original meaning of the text or the intent of the author. Nor are the meditations an endeavor to offer a theological treatise. Honestly, I am neither a theologian nor a biblical scholar, so if this is what you are after, you are probably fishing in the wrong stream. These meditations represent my own personal stories, musings, and words of advice that arise as I read these passages, reflecting on my own experience as a follower of Jesus over the years. I trust that you will find them refreshing, real, and helpful.

This book is organized into three parts, each part consisting of five meditations. Part 1, The Good Shepherd, contains meditations on protection, plenty, rest, serenity, and renewal. Part 2, The Gentle Guide, offers meditations on guidance, journey, courage, companionship, and correction. And Part 3, The Gracious Host, considers provision, blessing, overflow, grace, and home. I conclude with an attempt to bring the metaphors together in a meaningful way, demonstrating that God is a shepherd, a guide, and a host who offers us both kindness and hope as we do our best to love God and neighbor, and make our way home.

Each meditation follows a similar format: Introduction, Personal Story, Topical Reflection, Scripture, Some Practical Advice, and Questions for Reflection and Discussion. The meditations can be read as a personal devotional, for spiritual formation and discipleship instruction, or as a group activity. My advice is to gather a small group together and read each meditation. Then, listen carefully and prayerfully to each other, and let the discussion go where it will. And whether you read alone or in a group, end by identifying at least one way you see God working in your life and one specific thing you plan to do in response in the coming days. Write it down and follow through!

My hope for this book is that it will lead you from wherever you find yourself on the road between Psalm 21 to Psalm 22, on the road called life, to spend time in the green pastures and still waters of Psalm 23, soaking it up and reflecting on the character of God and the grace that is at work in us and through us. And my hope for you is that you will experience that profound love and companionship that God offers to each of us, and that you will truly come to see God as the good shepherd, the gentle guide, and the gracious host in your own life.

# PART I

# The Good Shepherd

The LORD is my shepherd; I shall not want. He makes me lie down in green pastures; He leads me beside still waters. He restores my soul.

—PSALM 23:1–3A

From the very first words of Psalm 23, the metaphor of the good shepherd is impossible to miss—beginning with the proclamation that "The LORD is my shepherd." Such a clear affirmation has deeply resonated with faithful readers for centuries. The first three verses suggest several ways that the good shepherd cares for the flock, for each of us, by offering protection, plenty, rest, serenity, and renewal. One chapter will be devoted to each of these ways that the good shepherd's presence is tangibly made manifest in our lives, giving us a chance to reflect both on God's goodness to us and how such kindness can be extended through us to our neighbors as well.

In these five chapters, we will think and examine together how God graciously shepherds our lives, and how our understanding of God's character and his work among us can be distorted when we misconstrue the metaphor of the shepherd, or it is hijacked by well-meaning friends or those with their own theological agendas. In addition, we will see how the metaphor of the good shepherd connects and leads naturally to the metaphor addressed in Part II, The Gentle Guide. Indeed, the work of a good shepherd and a gentle guide are intimately related, and we, all of us, are in need of divine care and loving guidance.

Let's get started!

# CHAPTER 1

## *The Lord is my Shepherd—Protection*

My sheep listen to my voice; I know them, and they follow me.
—JOHN 10:27

### Introduction

I met Paul Sharp for the first of many times in his office on the North Oval of the University of Oklahoma campus in Norman. He was the Regents Professor of Higher Education, having formally served as the university's president. After some small talk and a brief look at my résumé, he looked me squarely in the eyes, eyeball to eyeball as he was fond of saying, and said, "If you decide to join us this fall, I'm going to shepherd you through the program. You can count on it." Those were his exact words. He promised to see me through a rigorous PhD program in higher education. He went on to tell me about the faculty, the course work, and the support systems that were in place, but honestly, he had me at shepherd. I didn't know what I was getting myself into really, but if Paul Sharp would be my shepherd, I would listen to his voice and follow his advice. As it turned out, he was not shy about speaking into my life—always eyeball to eyeball. And for that, I will always be thankful.

I had Dr. Sharp (I never could call him Paul, even though he asked me to do so on several occasions) for the very first course in the program. Two weeks before the semester began, I received a syllabus, a plan for the course, in the mail. When I read through the assignments—three books to be read and a substantial paper written each week—I almost fainted.

"There must be some mistake. This is outrageous. No one can expect that much work for a single course. After all, I have a life to live, too!" Still, I came to the very first class meeting having read the first three books and struggled to write a ten-page paper suitable for submission. Joining me in the class were four other students. Before Dr. Sharp made his appearance, we students commiserated about the outlandish demands for the course and agreed that we would talk to Dr. Sharp about reducing the course load, particularly in light of the fact that we all were married and had jobs outside the university. I was designated to be the spokesperson.

Dr. Sharp entered the room with a burst of energy, looked the five of us over judiciously, and then flashed a big grin. He explained that somehow his course had been accidentally advertised as open to all university staff, and nearly fifty non-doctoral students were enrolled in the course. He said that he had to do something to thin the herd, as he put it, so he sent out the syllabus in advance. It worked. There was a rush to drop the course. Only the five of us were left, a skittish remnant. We all laughed nervously along with Dr. Sharp, and I decided to broach the subject and address the elephant in the room.

"That was a good strategy, Dr. Sharp," I began with a smile, carefully keeping my eyes locked on his crimson and cream silk tie, "so now the you have thinned the herd, can you give us the real assignment list for this semester? Clearly, you don't expect us to do all this work, do you?"

He looked over the class again, but this time it wasn't with a kind or friendly gaze. He nodded his head and pursed his lips but didn't say anything for what seemed like an eternity. Then, he leaned on the podium and began speaking in a low and deliberate voice. "Each of you were carefully screened and admitted into this doctoral program. There were other qualified applicants, but you five were deemed to be the best fit for the program. We saw real potential in you and had high hopes for each of you, but maybe we were wrong. Maybe we misjudged you. Honestly, I don't care how smart you are or how slick you think you are, if you are not fully committed to this program and prepared to work hard, you can leave now because I won't spend my time working with lazy or privileged students. Got that? It's all in or go home!"

I was both stunned and embarrassed by his forceful and direct manner. Of course, he was right. "Dr. Sharp," I began humbly, "I'm sorry for sounding glib, and to be honest the syllabus is a bit overwhelming, but I think I speak for all of us when I say, we're in—all in." My classmates nodded and murmured their agreement. "Ok, then," Dr. Sharp said with a smile, "let's get to work. Before we discuss the readings for this week, I believe that you have a paper for me. Right?" We turned in our papers, and faithfully did so every week throughout the semester. His shepherding had begun. I was all in.

About half way through the semester, Dr. Sharp asked if he could talk with me after class one evening. I sauntered down to his office and knocked on the door. He stepped into the hallway, carrying my latest paper in one hand and a red pen in the other. He looked me squarely in the eyes and asked, "Is this your best work, Patrick?" raising my paper and shaking it like a rag doll. "Well," I stammered in shock, "I've just started a new job and I've been traveling some and I've had a bad cold, too." It was the best excuse I could come up on short notice, and even now it sounds so very lame. In fact, it was. He nodded and said, "I know. I know. We all have problems, but you didn't answer my question, son. Is this your best work?" I looked down at the floor, and in a small, embarrassed voice replied, "No, I can do better." "I thought so," was his immediate response. "Don't you know that your work is your autograph—it says something about you? From now on, I only want to see your very best work. Are we clear?"

Of course, we were clear. For the rest of my doctoral program, and throughout my entire career in higher education, his words confronted and compelled me to always turn in my best work. It was a pointed rebuke, and a needed one—and he didn't have to tell me twice. To this day, I can hear his voice.

As I neared the end of my course work, I stopped by Dr. Sharp's office and asked him if he would consider serving as the chair of my doctoral committee. He said that he would, but only if I would add Dr. Jeffers to the committee. "Oh, Dr. Sharp, I'll add anyone you want, but please not Dr. Jeffers. Although brilliant, he is so esoteric and confusing that no one wants him to be on their research team." Dr. Sharp nodded and said, "I know, but if you want me, then you have to invite Dr. Jeffers, too. But don't worry, I'll protect you and see you through."

I wasn't too excited about this arrangement but I really wanted Dr. Sharp to oversee my efforts, so I agreed. All went smoothly until I met with the committee to defend my dissertation, the last step in the PhD process. About an hour into the meeting, Dr. Jeffers asked me a question about my use of a certain logical syllogism in my discussion of the intended outcomes of a liberal arts education. Honestly, I didn't know what he was asking me, so I asked him to repeat the question. Again, I was lost, so I asked if he could rephrase the question in some other way to help me understand. He looked a bit perturbed, and he raised his voice as he rephrased the question. I stared at the floor for a bit, then looked up and said, "Dr. Jeffers, I honestly don't know what you are asking me." I felt that my entire doctoral work was going out the window.

I sat there quietly, not knowing what to do, feeling like I had lost my way. Suddenly, Dr. Sharp leaned in and said, "Hell, Hugh, none of us know what you are asking. Please move on." And Dr. Jeffers did! The rest of the defense went smoothly, and I was congratulated that day as Dr. Allen for the first time. Dr. Sharp said that he would protect me, and he did.

My very last conversation with Dr. Sharp came a few months later. I was struggling with a career decision. Some professors in the department were pushing me to accept an offer to teach at a well-known research university in the Midwest. Honestly, it was an attractive offer, and my professors were convinced that it would help the departmental ratings, too. I stopped by Dr. Sharp's office and asked him for his advice.

He looked me straight in the eyes, eyeball to eyeball, and said, "Son, do what your heart tells you to do—what you feel called to do. Don't worry about those silly departmental ratings. We'll be fine here. It's your journey. Give your best efforts to something that counts for more than an impressive line on your resume." I did, and I have never looked back.

Paul Sharp promised to shepherd me through my doctoral program, and he did. He knew me—he pushed me. He saw more in me than I saw in myself. Truly, it was grace at work. To this very day, I can see his gaze and hear his voice—all in or go home, nothing but your best work, trust me, and trust your own heart, too. Jesus said, "My sheep listen to my voice; I know them, and they follow me" (John 10:27). Paul Sharp could say much the same thing. He was a good shepherd, providing direction and protection, sometimes from those around me and sometimes from my own foolishness and pride. Fortunately, I was smart enough to follow his voice—and to tell you the truth, I still do.

\* \* \*

In this chapter, we will examine the primary responsibility of a shepherd—to provide protection for the flock, for each one of us. As we will see, protection comes in many forms, sometimes protecting us from difficulties and dangers, sometimes protecting us for certain challenges and callings, and always protecting us in whatever circumstances and surroundings we find ourselves. Indeed, it is pure grace to affirm that the Lord is our shepherd, that he is a good shepherd, that he knows us, and we can hear his voice and follow him. Deo gratias!

## Shepherds

I think it is fair to begin with the acknowledgment that shepherds and sheep have not always been pictured in the most positive light. They could certainly use some image building and branding work, and I don't mean the kind of brands applied to the backsides of the sheep. After all, no one wants to be portrayed as a mindless animal following along in a mindless herd with no individual thoughts or convictions, or accused of being the keeper of such mindless animals. Clearly, shepherds were not a centerpiece of public society back in the day—or now, doing their work out in the fields, watching their flocks by day and by night. But King David knew a good deal about shepherds, having been one himself, and Jesus referred to his followers as his flock and noted that his sheep knew his voice. Surely, this was not a put-down in any sense of the word. It was a good thing to be in his flock, to hear his voice, to know and follow him. The metaphor of God as the good shepherd is found in Scripture more than forty times, and shepherds are mentioned well over one hundred times from Genesis to Revelation. The good shepherd metaphor communicated something very positive, a way to express care and courage and diligence.

And I think it fair to point out the angels appeared to lowly shepherds who were tending their flocks in the middle of the night, telling them of the birth of the Messiah—and neither the shepherds nor the baby Jesus were residing at the Holiday Inn in the town square at the time. They were the first on the scene to give witness to the birth and offer praise and adoration. In some divine way, I don't think this was just a coincidence. As outsiders, they would certainly be prime candidates to recognize and respond to a miraculous sign when they received one. After all, being on guard all alone in the middle of the night in fields far from the city lights would sharpen one's senses to recognize any unusual sights and sounds and heighten the ability to respond accordingly. It was the perfect place for such a message of hope, a place where shepherds tended their flocks in the darkness of night.

In our fast paced, technologically connected world, it is difficult to even think about what it means to be a shepherd. What do shepherds actually do? In essence, the job hasn't changed much in the past 500 years. Shepherds still live a simple life, devoted to their sheep. Their primary tasks are to attend to health issues, shearing (not skinning) of the sheep, keeping predators away, and flock welfare. According to the Mountain Plains Agricultural Service, a shepherd's primary responsibility is the safety and welfare of the flock—herding them to areas of good forage, grazing the animals, and keeping a watchful eye out for poisonous plants.

If it is true that "we all like sheep have gone astray" (Isa 53:6), and I think it is, then we all need a shepherd, a watchful eye concerned with our safety and welfare. We learn from Genesis that it is not good for anyone to be alone (Gen 2:18), and I would hasten to add that it is not good to decide to be your own shepherd either. We all need friends, mentors, and a shepherd, too, those who look after us, knowing us and caring for us, looking after our welfare even when we don't realize that we are in need, and that is all of us from time to time and some of us right now.

I am always moved when I think about the ancient redwood groves in California and Oregon. You don't see an isolated ancient redwood tree—they always grow in groves because they are so top-heavy that they can't put a tap root down far enough to support their massive weight. So, they put their roots out and grab on to each other. Standing side by side, a grove of redwoods can withstand rain and wind and fire for a thousand years or more. I believe that there is a lesson in this for each of us. We're top heavy, too, vulnerable to wind and rain and fire, so we need to reach out and hold on to others as if our lives depended on it, because in many respects, I believe they do. We all need a shepherd.

And the good news is that we don't have just any shepherd. We affirm with the writer of Psalm 23 that the LORD *is my shepherd* (1a). He knows us, so we listen intently to his voice and we follow him. And the icing of the cake is this—the Lord is a *good* shepherd. With a good shepherd comes provision, rest, serenity, renewal, direction, boundaries, trust, relationship, and correction, aspects that we will address in coming chapters, but there is one more dimension, protection, that I want us to consider before we look to Scripture for some insights into the nature of the good shepherd. Protection is at the very heart of what it means to be a good shepherd. As we will see, there are several dimensions of protection that come into play at different times in our lives. We need them all.

## Protection

When I think about protection, images of bodyguards, insurance policies, body armor, and outdoor shelters come quickly to mind, things that shield us from the elements and the vagaries of life, providing safety and security as we make our way. But I have come to see that there are more subtle forms of protection, too: a still small voice, a gentle rebuke from a trusted friend, even an open or closed door. Events that we often take as sheer coincidence or good fortune offer protection, too. Some may call it just being lucky. I call it providence.

We pray often to the good shepherd for protection in a variety of circumstances—for traveling mercies as we head out on a road trip, for a safe landing as the airline pilot struggles against a strong headwind, for a good test result from the lab, for a productive meeting with the boss, for the safe return of a loved one who is driving in bad weather, and for daily bread, to name just a few. There are many, many more. We are all looking for some peace and comfort, and most of us have uttered prayers, cries for help really, when feeling vulnerable, helpless, desperate, and afraid. When we are faced with painful and frightful things that are beyond our control, it disorients us and leaves us feeling exposed. In these situations, we are thankful that we have a good shepherd to run to. And in so many ways, our prayers are answered.

I ran across a prayer thanking God for our many blessings—known and unknown, remembered and forgotten. I think the same thing about protection, too. We pray for help in our time of need and our prayers are answered, but it somehow causes amnesia. We forget the many ways that we have experienced the protection of our shepherd in the midst of our difficulties, so the next time the wolf appears, we panic and cry out for help again. If the Lord is our shepherd, we can carry a deep sense of gratitude, mindful of the many protections we have received in the past in the midst of difficulties. Indeed, there are many—certainly more than we know or remember.

At the same time, I must confess that there are times when we do not see answers to our prayers, at least in a way we would want or recognize. God is silent, and seemingly absent. Questions about the whereabouts of God when tragedy strikes and why bad things happen to good people, even to us, have vexed humanity for as long as we have been on this earth. While there are many simple and simplistic answers to these heartfelt questions, few are deeply satisfactory. And I won't muddy the waters by trying to explain different theological approaches to these questions, but simply confess that I honestly do not know. It is a mystery to me, but it doesn't stop me from praying and asking for divine guidance and protection. What I can affirm is that even in the darkest hours in the middle of the night, the Lord is my shepherd. I'll stand firm on that reality even when the wolves have encircled the flock and the shepherd is nowhere in sight. We will examine this question further in the Scripture section below. Suffice it here to say, God has not promised that we will avoid all suffering, disappointment, and pain in this life. Rather, God has promised that he will neither leave us nor forsake us. He will be with us in our suffering. He is our shepherd.

Certainly, we can see God's protection for us in our own lives, particularly when we look back at past events. Have you ever been disappointed by a closed door, perhaps being turned down for a new job, only to look back a year or so later to realize that you were spared a painful or disastrous experience? That's a form of God's protection. And I believe that God protects us through open doors, through the sound of a still, small voice, through the words and warnings of good friends, through the wisdom and advice of mentors, and through our own intuition and experience. God protects us by shielding us from external threats, and from our own selfish and impulsive actions, too.

And protection has a future trajectory as well. God doesn't only protect us *from* things, he protects us *for* things, too. In many ways, I can look back at my life and see times that I was headed in the wrong direction, making choices that I would certainly come to regret later on. Through a variety of means—good friends, wise counsel, my own conscience and intuition, and fear, to name only four—I avoided serious blunders that would have wreaked havoc with my plans for the future. God protected my future from my own imperfect inclinations. And if I am honest, I can look back to a few decisions that I made despite knowing better, and to this day I regret those decisions. I wish I had listened to the shepherd.

In addition, even in the midst of painful situations, God protected my spirit. The experiences were horrible, but my spirit was not broken. And now as I look back, I can say that I wouldn't be writing this book with the same passion and insight without going through those experiences, as painful as they were at the time. Through it all, God sheltered my spirit, and I hope my writing bears witness that swimming in deep water and drowning are not the same thing.

At the end of the day, I have come to believe that we are surrounded by the protection of the good shepherd. That fact doesn't remove us from the human race or make us immune from pain and suffering, but we journey with the promise that God is with us, watching over us, providing and protecting in ways known and unknown, remembered and forgotten. Indeed, the Lord is our shepherd, and he is good.

## Scripture

In this section, we will look at two instances where protection was offered to faithful followers, and to unfaithful followers, too. We'll look first at the stories of Samuel and Eli (1 Sam 3), a story about hearing and responding to the voice of the shepherd. Then, we'll draw from the story of the pillar of cloud and fire that led the Israelites out of Egypt (Exod 13) to consider what might be at work when we do not sense God's protection or presence during tough and terrible times. As you will see, these Old Testament stories have much to teach each of us about the protection of the good shepherd.

## Samuel and Eli

Samuel served as a transitional leader between the time of the judges and the reign of kings. As a young boy, he ministered before the Lord under the tutelage of Eli, a high priest of Shiloh. "In those days the word of the LORD was rare; there were not many visions" (1 Sam 3:1a). One night, Samuel heard a voice calling out to him, so he quickly got up and ran to Eli, waking him from a sound sleep. Eli assured the young boy that he had not called to him and sent him back to bed. The same voice called out a second, and then a third time. Each time Samuel ran to Eli. On the third occasion, it finally dawned on Eli that it was the Lord's voice that Samuel was hearing and instructed him that if he heard the voice again, to simply say, "Speak, for your servant is listening" (1 Sam 3:10b). The voice came a fourth time, and Samuel did as he was instructed.

In the morning, Eli asked Samuel what the Lord had said to him. Samuel was reluctant to tell him since it was not good news, but Eli insisted. So, Samuel shared that God was displeased with the way Eli's sons were using their position as priests to line their own pockets, to fill their stomachs with the best cuts of meat offered as sacrifices, and to take advantage of women who served at the entrance of the tent of meeting. Actually, it was the third time that Eli had received such a message from the Lord, and sadly, as with the other two warnings, his sons continued their reprehensible behavior. Eli's own story ends with the news that his two sons were killed in battle. He was an old man, ninety-eight years old, blind, and overweight. He leaned back in disbelief and fell off his chair, resulting in a broken neck. Eli died on the spot.

There are several insights we can draw from this sad story. First, in those days, much like the present day, the word of the Lord was difficult to recognize. Samuel didn't recognize the Lord's voice even though he heard it several times. He needed someone to help him discern the voice that was calling out to him and respond appropriately. Given all the banal voices and noise in our world today, younger people in particular need mentors and trusted friends to help them discern and respond when God is speaking to them, and to tell the difference between God's voice and groundless noise so prevalent in a culture propelled and dominated by social media. Whatever else Eli did that displeased the Lord, he did help Samuel recognize God's voice and respond, "Speak, for your servant is listening." Hopefully, we can learn to listen and respond in the same way even today.

Second, even though Eli taught Samuel to hear God's voice and respond in obedience, he ignored the voice himself. God rebuked Eli at least three times, warning him of the consequences for his entire family and legacy if his sons kept on misusing their positions as priests. He never stopped them, and it all ended in tragedy. Very sad, indeed. Clearly, even when we are trying to help others discern God's leading in their lives, it is incumbent upon each of us to listen and obey, too. It is so easy for us to dispense spiritual advice about hearing God; it is much harder to receive such correction ourselves, even when we are lovingly confronted with our own reckless attitudes and behaviors, often more than once.

Finally, I think it is important to note that even though Samuel received his training in the midst of a very dysfunctional system, a spiritual organization that had lost its way, he emerged as a powerful spiritual leader, prepared to bridge the transition from the time of judges to the reign of kings. In fact, he was the one who anointed Saul as Israel's first king. God's voice protected Samuel *from* disillusionment and *for* leadership. It is good to know that God is at work in our lives, too, protecting us even when it is difficult to discern, something we will see in the story of the pillar of cloud and fire.

## The Pillar of Cloud and Fire

We find an interesting portrayal of God's protection in the Old Testament book of Exodus: "By day the LORD went ahead of them in a pillar of cloud to guide them on their way and by night in a pillar of fire to give them light, so that they could travel by day or night. Neither the pillar of cloud by day nor the pillar of fire by night left its place in front of the people" (Exod 13:21–22). As the children of Israel left their homes in Egypt, heading for the promised land, it would be difficult to imagine a more tangible sign of God's protection—a pillar of cloud by day and a pillar of fire by night. It must have been reassuring to the Israelites, especially since they knew that the Egyptians might reconsider and come after them. And, of course, as it turned out, they had much to be worried about. The dust raised by Pharaoh's army could be seen in their rearview mirrors just as they reached the shores of the Red Sea. They were boxed in, between the devil and the deep blue sea.

To make matters even worse, this is what happened next: "Then the angel of God, who had been traveling in front of Israel's army, withdrew and went behind them. The pillar of cloud also moved from in front and stood behind them . . ." (Exod 14:19–20a). Just in their hour of deepest need, it seemed to the Israelites that God was no longer leading. In fact, he was nowhere to be seen. Fear and despair prevailed, but that was not the end of the story. The pillar of cloud brought darkness to the Egyptian army, so they didn't advance, and the pillar of fire provided light for the Israelites to work through the night to prepare for crossing the sea. So, God was in protection mode even when they could not see the pillars. He was protecting them from something (the Egyptian army) and for something (a new start). He had their backs.

I think there is a lesson in this story for all of us. It is so good when God's leading is visible and discernible, but just because we don't see or sense God's hand of protection, it does not mean that we have been abandoned. I like to think of it this way—when nothing is happening, something is happening. God has our backs. We might not be able to see it, but God is with us, protecting us from known and unknown dangers, for the journey ahead of us and in the midst of our difficulties, too.

## Some Practical Advice

Before we conclude with some questions for reflection and discussion, let me offer just a few words of practical advice as we reflect on the protection of the good shepherd.

### Stop and Listen

First, stop and listen. It sounds simple, but it isn't. It is so easy to go through our busy days and not even stop for a moment and consider listening to what God has to say to us. So, stop and listen. Make an appointment with yourself to take fifteen minutes and do nothing other than to say, "Speak, for your servant is listening." Then listen! That's a good place to start. And as you go through the day, listen for God's voice. With intention, you will hear it.

### Follow God's Voice

And when you hear God's voice, follow it. Jesus said that his sheep knew his voice and followed it (John 10:27). If you are unclear about who is speaking or what you are being told to do, talk to a mentor, close friend, or spiritual advisor—someone you trust to help you discern the message and find your way forward. No need to do this alone.

### First a Friend, Then a Prophet

Also, if you are impressed to speak into someone's life, speak through a relationship when you can. I must confess that I am a bit wary when someone I don't really know comes up to me and delivers "a word from God" for me. I do suppose that God can speak to us in that way, but it makes much more sense to me when God speaks through someone with whom I have a trusting relationship. The former feels a bit too much like spiritual grandstanding to me, while the later feels much more invested and caring. To be clear, I am not saying that you should not speak into the lives of others. No, you should if you are so led, but I think the place to start is to establish real and deep relationships with others, then allow the spirit to speak through you as you share life together. In my experience, when you speak friend to friend rather than as a stranger or prophet, the chances that the message will be received and embraced are much, much better. And you are there for the journey after the message is delivered.

### Rely on God's Promises, Not Your Feelings

Finally, when you think about God's protection in your life, don't let your feelings deceive you or drive your understanding of God's protection. Let's be honest. Sometimes it is difficult to see God at work or hear God's voice. I've been there myself, and some of us may be there right now. Remember, when nothing is happening, something is happening. Rely on the promise of protection, not your feelings. "As the mountains surround Jerusalem, so the LORD surrounds his people both now and forever" (Ps 125:2). Amen.

## Conclusion

Everyone needs a shepherd, and it is not a good idea to try to be your own. We affirm that the Lord is our shepherd, a good shepherd. We are known, we hear the shepherd's voice, and we follow. At the end of the day, often when we look back, we see the protection of the good shepherd—protection *from* things that come our way and from ourselves, too, protection *for* opportunities yet to be realized, and always *in* whatever difficulties and wherever we are. Indeed, we are surrounded by God's protection even as the mountains surround Jerusalem, both now and forever. This knowledge cannot help but bring both hope and courage. Thanks be to God.

## Questions for Reflection and Discussion:

1. Think back to a time when you experienced God's protection. Was it protection from, protection in, or protection for? Would you say it was directly from God, or was it mediated by someone, perhaps a close friend, mentor, or spiritual director?

2. When you consider the circumstances and schedule of your life, what is the biggest impediment to setting aside time to listen to God each day? Do you set aside at least fifteen minutes each day for a listening session? If not, could you?

3. Have you ever felt impressed to speak into someone's life? Was it a close friend, acquaintance, or stranger? How did it go?

4. Are you inclined to fear or worry when you do not sense God's direction and protection? Can you recall a time when in hindsight God was at work even though you could not see or feel it?

5. How do you discern God's voice and direction from the many voices and constant noise present in our culture? What advice would you give to someone who desires to keep spiritually centered and directed?

# Psalm 23

*The Lord is my shepherd . . .*

# CHAPTER 2

## *I Shall Not Want—Plenty*

> Too often we visit the well of divine abundance
> with a teacup instead of a bucket.
>
> —ELINOR MACDONALD

### Introduction

I grew up in a small town in central Michigan. My parents provided my three brothers and me a caring and nurturing home. Growing up in a neighborhood with more than a dozen World War II war babies, life was full. There was always something to do—ball games, hiking, fishing, digging holes in the garden, and constructing venues for Olympic track meets in the back yard. And we played in the summer until long after dark; first playing hide-and-go-seek, then bloody murder. I honestly can't think of a bad day, even when it rained.

That is, until I hit the seventh grade. In those days, that was the start of junior high, a merging of the three elementary schools in our town. All of a sudden, there were new kids in my classes and sports activities. Certainly, we had much better baseball and basketball teams. The competition was stiff, so I had to work hard and practice to make the teams. It made me a better player, for sure. Hard work and practice tend to do that in just about any activity.

However, there was a downside to the merging of the three elementary schools, something that I doubt anyone in my small town, certainly my parents, expected would happen. For the first time in my short, insulated life, I experienced what sociologists call social stratification, a kind of social differentiation whereby a society groups people into socio-economic strata based upon their occupation, income, wealth, and social status. My mother would simply call it the formation of a pecking order. We were the chickens.

I was taught from an early age that "people are just people," and we were expected to treat everyone with kindness and dignity, no matter where they came from or what their parents did for a living. All of us, my parents would tell us, are children of God. Unfortunately, the children of God in junior high had other ideas. Status was granted to those who wore "store-bought" clothes. All my clothes were homemade, and many were hand-me-downs, too. Status was also given to those who brought their lunch in a fancy bag with sandwiches made with Wonder Bread. My sandwiches were made with homemade bread baked by my mother. We couldn't afford such luxuries, and others in the class noted the difference. And my father didn't work in the bank or own his own business. Somehow that reflected on me, too. I wasn't sure how or why, but I felt it nonetheless, especially when I was not invited to certain swimming pool parties held on the other side of town in Orchard Hills or West Gate, the closest thing in our town to a desired address. Our house was very near the railroad tracks on the other side of town.

All this social stratification took its toll on me, and it was difficult to shake. Later, when I transferred to a denominational college before my junior year, I arrived with two dress shirts, a blazer, and a matching tie, all made by my mother. Imagine my shock when my classmates pulled up in new cars and unloaded box after box after box of clothes and stereo equipment. I didn't fit in, feeling like I had just arrived from another planet.

When I graduated college, found a job, and began to earn some money—making more in that first year than my father would ever make in any year of his life, I made a furious attempt to make up for lost time. I bought a full closet of new clothes. I had a suit for every work day of the month and a tie to match. I bought a new car every year, and traveled around the world. I bought jewelry, expensive golf equipment, a racket club membership, and a frequent new house almost on a whim. As I look back, of course, I can see now that I was chasing after acceptance and approval, thinking and hoping that having things would fill my cup. Actually, it did socially, but my spirit was empty. Reciting Psalm 23 rang hollow, "I shall not want." To be honest, I wanted everything and I just couldn't buy enough fast enough. It took some years to understand that there is no end to this acquisition game unless you decide not to play anymore. Thankfully, that's what I did.

However, I replaced this "buy-everything-you-want" strategy with an equally insidious one—the "it-will-look-good-on-my-resume" game. This game is quite simple. Every career and professional decision you make is predicated on getting something new on your resume—a promotion, a presentation, a committee appointment, a publication, a better job. The longer the resume, the more professional status you have. During the middle years of my career, I was a resume builder, and it was impressively long. What a good feeling it was to send it along with a cover letter when I applied for yet another job. I was building my resume as if it represented my self-worth—my life.

It took some time, but I finally came to the realization that my work and my character would speak for itself. I didn't have to pad my resume or flaunt a new job title. I suppose a good deal of this realization came as the result of maturity and going through some tough times. Now when I recite Psalm 23, I sincerely agree, "The LORD is my shepherd; I shall not want" (1). My value as a person is not determined by what I own or by what I have done, but rather by the kind of person I am, attempting each day to love God with everything I have and my neighbor as if my life depended on it. It is not about having or doing, but about being the kind of person that pleases the good shepherd, following his voice. It is living a simple, sincere, and serene life with all the courage and compassion and kindness possible. I shall not want anything else, and honestly, I don't.

\* \* \*

## Chasing Plenty

You can see from my own story, coming to terms with what you have and who you are is not always easy, and it usually takes time to distinguish that they are not one and the same. Yet, the insatiable materialism that surrounds us, the ever-present advertising that overwhelms us, and the incessant competition for things to give meaning to our lives that dominate our culture speak to just the opposite. We are told—you are what you have, you are what you do, and your identity is the sum total of what you have accumulated—so buy, do, and be! This is a sad, sad reality we face every day. Our worth as a person is measured, the message goes, by these things.

And then to add insult to misery, the pervasive message continues—it is not only what you have and what you do, but it is also the way you look. Having, doing, and looking a certain way are the indicators of success, and these keys to success are what is important because they will make you feel important. All you need to do is watch almost any thirty-minute television or cable program, and this idea of success will be promoted, often more than once.

Of course, there are several serious problems with this approach to life. For starters, no matter how much you accumulate and pad your resume, there are always others who have more and have done more than you. It's a race you simply can't win. If we determine our personal worth by which rung of the ladder we cling to, we will come to the realization sooner or later that there are always other rungs to climb. The ladder has no top rung. It is ultimately an exercise in futility, because no matter how hard we work at it, we will end up on the short end of the competition. The only way I see to honestly deal with a competition such as this is to simply choose not to play the game. That's a choice we can make.

But it is hard, isn't it? We all want to be liked, to be "in" with a group, our group, to look good, to be the one with the store-bought bread sandwich. No one really wants to be left out or feel differently, certainly not in middle school, and most of us carry this sensitivity most of our lives. However, with time and distance, call it maturity and wisdom, it becomes clear that there is much more to this life than possessing a good-looking sandwich. May we be wise enough to avoid the accumulation game in a land of plenty. Hopefully, the first words of Psalm 23 speak plainly to each of us. When we have the Lord as our shepherd, we have no need to want—particularly if what we are told that we should want, even need, are things that will give us status and prop up our sagging egos. Kingdom values don't work that way. Rather than affluence, appearance, and achievement, values that if chased will ultimately dry you up like an old leaf, the life-giving values of the kingdom are character, compassion, and community. When we focus on this reality, we shall not want.

Yet another difficulty comes when we compete with others, comparing ourselves to what they have or how they look or what they have done. It is always a mistake to judge the quality of our insides by looking at the outsides of others. Far too often, if truth be told, many very successful-looking persons are simply wearing a mask, hiding a deep emptiness inside, trying desperately to fill it up with something—anything. Deep down, there is a tacit recognition that in the "kingdom of thingdom," the emperor has no clothes, so don't be fooled by appearances.

Perhaps the saddest aspect of this cultural materialism is that it has taken root in our churches, too. We invite successful business persons to speak to us and lead our weekend retreats. They tell a wonderful story of God's guidance, blessing them as they have built a profitable business and accumulated a good deal of wealth or distinction of one kind or another. It seems to me that a plumber or a custodian or a farm worker are rarely, if ever, invited to speak about God's faithfulness to them and with them. Why does someone have to be financially successful to be noteworthy? Now, please hear me. There is nothing particularly wrong with being successful, or being wealthy for that matter. However, the message that is often communicated, sometimes unconsciously and sometimes consciously, is that material wealth *is* a sign of God's blessing in our lives, and it is just a small step from there to suggest that if we were only more faithful, God would bless our lives even more, too, and by blessings we mean having more things and getting better jobs—the material signs of God's favor.

Of course, this is more than misguided; it is simply wrong. As we read in 1 Samuel 16:7b, "The LORD does not look at the things people look at. People look at the outward appearance, but the LORD looks at the heart." Isn't this good advice for all of us? Certainly, our identity is in Christ, not in our wealth or our social status or our job. For that, I am truly thankful, because such things can come and go like the wind. On the other hand, God's economy turns so many things on their heads, and understanding plenty is one of them. The key, it seems to me, is to be mindful of the lavish abundance of God's grace in our lives, and the wealth of spiritual resources that are available to each one of us. When we focus our lives on abundance rather than on plenty—at least on having plenty of things—we can join with the writer of Psalm 23 in affirming, "I shall not want." We can do so because we have all we will ever need. Remember, we are called to be faithful, not successful, especially given how our culture (and so many of our churches, even our church leaders) define success and understand plenty.

## Recognizing Abundance

*Abundance* is a wonderful word. In so many ways, I like it better than the word *plenty*, because abundance suggests a wider embrace of what truly matters in life, the resources that are available to us, the things that fill our spiritual cups, and what it means to not be in want—whether we are making our way in a land of plenty or we find ourselves in a desert place of one kind or another. The key, it seems to me, is to recognize the spiritual abundance that is available to each of us, that surrounds us and follows us, regardless of where we are on our journey or the difficulty of the pathway ahead. As we, all of us, make our way toward home, we do so in the full and abundant supply of God's grace and goodness, whether we know it or not.

So, what does a full and abundant supply mean and what does it look like? For starters, a full and abundant supply means more than ample. Ample is good, but abundance is more than ample; it means overly sufficient, generous, even lavish. Many of us are familiar with the story Jesus told about the farmer who was out sowing seeds, often called the parable of the Sower (Luke 8). The seeds are the word of God, Jesus explains to his disciples, and the focus of the story turns quickly to the different types of soil on which the seeds fall, and the success of the crop, we can infer, depends largely on the quality of the soil. According to the story, seeds need good soil to grow and mature. This is all well and good, but I honestly think that the story turns away from the sower and to the seeds a bit too quickly. Remember, the name of the story is the parable of the Sower, not the parable of the Seed. When I read this parable, I picture a farmer who is generously, lavishly, abundantly—even wildly—sowing seeds, not just in the good soil but all over the place. To me, it is a wonderful picture of God's desire to overwhelm our lives with goodness and grace, abundantly flinging possibilities to us regardless of the soil around us. At the end of the story, Jesus said, "Whoever has ears to hear, let them hear" (Luke 8:8b). I think that would include all of us.

And we should not only hear but respond accordingly. Far too often, we approach the repository of God's love and grace, a veritable ocean, with a teacup instead of a bucket. We hesitate to ask God for help with the little things in our lives, like getting our child to sleep or a good night's rest ourselves, having a healthy and productive conversation with a friend, successfully painting the kitchen, or making a meaningful connection at church. How could God be interested in such small things? The answer is simply this: The God of the universe has an ocean of resources available to you, so ask! Come with a bucket, and don't be shy. Keep your teacup on display as a reminder of how inadequate your vision was for what God had in store for your life.

So, when we speak of an ocean of God's abundant resources for us, what are we talking about? Let me list just a few: the gifts and abilities we have been given, our own intuition and the still small voice that speaks to us, the wisdom we draw from our own experiences and from Scripture, the opportunities before us, and the passions, dreams, and desires we carry. Also, the relationships we have that offer guidance, instruction, fellowship, and opportunities for service as we journey together. Often, these resources can best be found within the context of the local church. That is why I advocate that we all find a local faith community that really needs help, and then roll up our sleeves and show up anytime we can. Rather than looking for the church that best addresses our needs, why not look for the church that most needs us? Bring a bucket, maybe two. Get involved. Start flinging seeds of your own. View weekly attendance and service as spiritual practices, activities that over time will shape us in ways heretofore unimagined because we are tapping into the storehouse of God's abundance. And as we look back, we will see the hand of God at work all over our lives, the abundance of blessings secured through a lifetime of faithful service. What could be better than that?

## Learning to Abide

There is one additional idea that suggests itself when we reflect on the affirmation—I shall not want. In addition to understanding the material trap of chasing plenty and recognizing the gift of God's abundant resources all around us and available to us, especially in our local faith community, it is also necessary to learn to abide. Let's unpack this idea a bit before looking to Scripture for added insight, and then considering a few words of practical advice as we end this chapter.

In the Gospel of John, Jesus tells his disciples that he is the vine and reminds them that they are the branches. They are to abide (or remain) in him, and if they do, they will bear good fruit. Apart from the vine, however, they can do nothing, meaning that they will not bear fruit of any useful kind (15:5). I think this is a word for all of us. The good news is that there is a vine, and the even better news is that we are not it! We are not called to be the entire vine. Thank God. Instead, we are the branches. Our summons is to abide, to stay connected to the vine and bear good fruit. We are to abide in him and love each other. That we can do.

In the same passage, Jesus also affirms that he is the true vine (John 15:1). I think that this is a key aspect in learning to abide. Where does your identity come from? You see, the Jews thought that they were the true vine. They understood their identity as being God's chosen people, set apart and special in the eyes of God. Here, Jesus confronts that worldview and simply affirms that we draw our identity from him. He is the true vine, and we are the branches who draw our identity, our strength, our nourishment, and our connection from him. As we learn to abide in him, we identify ourselves as followers of Jesus, and we affirm that we shall not want.

The other important message from John 15 about learning to abide is that we will be pruned to be even more fruitful (2). Yikes! I'm not sure that being pruned sounds much like fun, and many times, to be honest, it isn't, but if we want to learn to abide, then some unproductive values, ideas, behaviors, attitudes, and relationships have to go. They need to be pruned. If not, they will simply draw away life-giving resources that should be going into the production of good fruit. Strange as it may at first sound, pruning and abiding go hand in hand.

At the end of the day, when we affirm that we shall not want, it is a statement about our understanding of God and our connection to the living vine, and it is a testimony, too. I am told that the Amish do not pray for rain, despite their steadfast understanding that God is interested and active in their daily lives. Instead, they wait for rain, and when it comes, they are thankful. I think this picture of faith offers a glimpse into what it means to abide. Such abiding is much more than a blind submission to that which is beyond our influence and control. We are not simply helpless puppets subject to the whims of the master puppeteer or the vagaries of life. It is not a blind, hopeless, helpless fatalism, but rather a deep and restful faith in a God who is present and cares deeply for each of us, who is good, loving, gracious, and kind—and as we learn to abide, we shall not want.

## Scripture

When we look to the wisdom of Scripture to reflect on the affirmation that we have all we need, that we will not live in want, there are literally hundreds of passages that we could examine that speak to the folly of chasing plenty, to the gift of recognizing abundance all around us, and to the contentment that comes when we learn to abide in God's presence. However, in this portion of the chapter, I would like for us to look briefly at just two passages, one from the Lord's Prayer and the other from the story of the Prodigal Son.

## The Lord's Prayer

When his disciples asked Jesus to teach them to pray, he offered them a simple approach found in Matthew's gospel. In the prayer, we find these two affirmations: "your kingdom come, your will be done . . ." (6:10). I have heard sermons that focus directly on the second of the two affirmations, your will be done, suggesting that we have little to do other than to surrender our will, our desires, our hopes and dreams, our very self, in a selfless kind of fatalism that says that God is in total control and our job is to simply surrender ourselves and take whatever comes full in the face. After terrible tragedies and even national elections, I have heard people say that God is in control, and we have to just sit back and take it. It is out of our hands.

I think that this approach, while quite popular, is a bit shortsighted. Does God really want to pull all the strings and have us bob up and down like puppets in a carnival show? I don't think so. Rather than saying that God is in control, implying that there is nothing we can or should do, it's out of our hands, I prefer to say in difficult and terrible times—Jesus is Lord. In the prayer that Jesus taught his disciples to pray, "your will be done" immediately follows "your kingdom come." This, it seems to me, is by no mere coincidence. They are intimately connected. We are to pray for, look for, and work for the coming of the kingdom here on earth, and as we do, we pray "your will be done," seeing that the coming of the kingdom *is* his will.

And what is God's will that is to be done as the kingdom comes? This, it seems to me, is no secret or mystery. We are to live justly, love mercy, and walk humbly with God (Mic 6:8). We are to love God with everything we have, and love our neighbors as if life together depended on it (Matt 22:37, Mark 12:30–31, Luke 10:27). And we are called to be holy in all we do (1 Pet 1:15). As we do these things, we will help to usher in the kingdom—on earth as it is in heaven. As we learn to abide in him, to draw our identity from him, and stay connected to him, we will learn to abide even more, to exercise a steadfast faith that Jesus is lord, while also actively leaning in to the task of bringing in the kingdom right where we live. God does not want us to be empty. God wants us to be full—full of love, full of hope, full of dreams, and full of passion. Ultimately, God calls us to be a faithful presence in our own neighborhoods, loving God and others with all we have and are, not passive puppets on display, waiting for the next string to be pulled.

## The Prodigal Son

This is a story familiar to most of us (Luke 15:11–32). To get a picture of the prodigal son, all we have to do is look at some of the synonyms for *prodigal* in the dictionary: wasteful, reckless, extravagant, self-indulgent, uncontrolled, dissolute, and dissipated. None of us would want to be described this way. Sadly, it was a result of chasing plenty, trying desperately to fill the emptiness he felt inside. The prodigal was given plenty, and he squandered it in a dismal attempt to be somebody by buying everything in sight. He wanted more and more and more. In the end, chasing plenty landed him in a pig pen, and the emptiness was still there—now on steroids.

The son decided to go back home and try to get a job as a day laborer, but his father wouldn't hear of it. He put a robe around his shoulders, a ring on his finger, and threw him a first-rate party. The prodigal came back to his father with a teacup and the father doused him with an ocean of love and forgiveness. Abundant resources were all around him, but he could not see it or thought he no longer deserved them. There's a lesson here for all of us, too, as we learn to see that abundance of God's grace and goodness all around us.

## Some Practical Advice

Before we end this chapter with some questions for reflection and discussion, let me offer just a few words of practical advice, tangible ways to affirm that when the Lord is our shepherd, we shall not want.

## Dream Big Dreams

To start, dream big dreams. Recognize the abundant possibilities that surround us. In my role as an academic dean, I would meet with faculty who were interested in pursuing a grant. Often, they would ask, "How much do you think we can get?" I would smile and say, "Let's not ever be accused of thinking too small. Start by asking for what we need, and do not limit the proposal to what we think we can receive." That's good advice for us all. Dream big. Imagine outlandish possibilities. God will not be offended. Bring a bucket or two. Leave the teacup in the kitchen cabinet.

## Be Mindful of the Small Stuff

And as you dream big dreams, ask God for help in the little things in life, too, and keep on asking. Make it a spiritual practice to talk to God about the needs and concerns you have, even, perhaps especially, the everyday happenings in your life. There are no spiritual penalties for persistence. I think we often fail to persist because we can't quite imagine that the God of the universe could be interested in our little corner of the world, in dealing with a headache or getting your child to get a good night's rest. Give God the opportunity to surprise you. Ironically, one aspect of thinking too small is thinking that small things are not worth mentioning to God. Even as we dream big dreams, it is important to be mindful of the little ways that God is interested and active in our lives.

## Find a Church and Dig In

Find a church that really needs you. Consider it a spiritual practice to attend regularly, establish authentic relationships, and serve often. Over time, you will be shaped and formed in ways that you couldn't anticipate or imagine. And stay put—formation takes time. Approach church attendance as a pilgrim, one who is on a journey to a holy place rather than as a consumer. For so many of us, finding a church home is really hard, even painful, so we bounce around from one church to another, enjoying the attention that comes with being new rather than doing the hard work of making friends, developing caring relationships, and getting involved. Find a faith community and dig in. Make that your holy place.

### Prune the Branches

Finally, find a quiet place and take an hour or two, even a day, to evaluate your spiritual life. Are there unproductive branches that are not bearing fruit? Ask God to highlight them, and begin to think prayerfully about how they might be pruned. When I did so just a few weeks ago, it became clear to me that I was carrying some anger and resentment from a past work relationship that needed to be pruned. As God dealt with me about my own unproductive behavior, I realized that I was still receiving monthly emails and newsletters from that organization, and I fumed and fussed about almost everything I read. So, I unsubscribed, pruning away some unnecessary irritations that led to unproductive emotions. That was easy. Now, God is dealing with me about extending forgiveness. To be honest, that's not been as easy and I'm still working on it. In my experience, new growth comes slowly, steadily, and surely after pruning, and with new growth comes good fruit. I so much want my life to be the bearer of good fruit. I know you do, too.

## Conclusion

I shall not want. In so many ways, these words from Psalm 23 seem unrealistic—even naïve. Surely, it's not possible to live without wanting things, is it? Isn't life all about having all our needs and most of our wants satisfied? Clearly, that's what our culture tells us every single day in so many ways. However, in this chapter we examined the benefits of opting out of the "chasing plenty" game, and the rich blessings that are ours when we recognize the spiritual abundance that surrounds us and we learn to abide in Christ, even when it requires a bit of pruning or the removal of a branch or two, perhaps especially so.

As we close this meditation, we acknowledge our deep desire to sink our roots deep in the soil of God's love and care, to be connected to the true vine, and to be productive followers of the one who calls us to be holy. As Jesus told his disciples, "If you remain in me and I in you, you will bear good fruit" (John 5:15). I believe that he was speaking to each of us, too. And when we abide in him, the good shepherd, we shall not want.

## Questions for Reflection and Discussion:

1. What would be your version of the "homemade bread sandwich story" that opened this chapter? What did you want so much but when possessed, it didn't live up to its billing? Do you still deal with this issue?

2. Which dominant value from our culture is most attractive and enticing for you—appearance, achievement, or affluence? Why so?

3. How might you recalibrate your priorities to practice the dominant values in God's economy—character, compassion, and community? Which of these is most in need of some spiritual attention? What would be a good first step or two for you to take?

4. If you were to be accused of thinking too small about spiritual things, would it be about your big dreams or about the little everyday aspects of your life?

5. As you reflect on this chapter, is there some pruning that needs to take place? Are there some unproductive branches in your life? What is a productive first step?

## Psalm 23

*The LORD is my shepherd; I shall not want. . . .*

## CHAPTER 3

## *He Makes Me Lie Down In Green Pastures—Rest*

> Rest and be thankful.
> —WILLIAM WORDSWORTH

### Introduction

On Sunday afternoons, after church and Sunday dinner (usually roast chicken, mashed potatoes, biscuits, gravy, corn or green beans, and a Jell-O salad of some sort), my three brothers and I were banished to our rooms for a Sunday afternoon nap. We were to rest in our beds and be still for at least an hour. Honestly, it seemed like an entire afternoon. I used to think that my mother really wanted us to take a nap, but as I look back at all the kinetic activity that took place in our very small house, I'm now sure that my parents just wanted an hour of peace and quiet before preparing for another busy week. I rarely if ever went to sleep. Instead I read a book or looked at a scouting or sports magazine. Sleep was out of the question. I went through the motions, but my mind was never at rest.

At scout camp, we were also sent to our tents each afternoon for a "stand down hour." Our leaders told us that such times were necessary to recharge our batteries, given all the activities that went on during the day (and sometimes well into the night). We didn't listen. How could we sleep when we needed to learn how to tie a bowline knot, the king of knots, and practice our secret hand signals in the event that we came under attack from a bear or the Girl Scout troop from the other side of the lake? We were simply too busy learning new things to rest. By the end of camp, I was totally exhausted, unable to stay awake even when we stopped at the Tasty Freeze in Mt. Pleasant for some ice cream on the way home. My parents could not arouse me from my half-sleep coma, and as far as I can remember it was the only time in my life that I willingly passed up a sweet treat of any kind.

In high school, our basketball coach told us that it would be good to take a short nap right after school on game days. We needed to be rested for the big games ahead. I dutifully did what my coach advised, but I just couldn't sleep. I was dreaming about the cheering crowd and my hoped-for exploits at the game. My mind was too full of anticipation and dreams to rest. Instead, I listened to the radio and said a prayer or two. I often became quite religious when facing big challenges—and possible embarrassments.

While in the midst of my professional career as an academic administrator, I was simply too busy for a nap—even on weekends. Too busy, that is, until I faced some very difficult days at the university where I worked. I was going through a divorce, and several ministers on the board of trustees were pushing for my resignation, hoping that I would simply go away. It seems I was an embarrassment to them. All this led to a severe bout of depression. Some days, I was barely able to put one foot in front of the other. And I slept a lot, too, but not a restful sleep. Rather, it was my chosen mode of escape. I was empty, and sleep passed the hours but did little to restore my broken spirit.

Fast forward to today. As you read this story, I am happily retired—and I nap nearly every day, sometimes twice. I have come to the realization that a nap is a good discipline, a regular part of my life. I get tired a bit quicker now, and a nap renews both body and spirit. Resting is an integral part of my daily routine. Rest is good!

I think there are spiritual applications to draw from this story as well. The writer of Psalm 23 affirms that the good shepherd "makes me lie down in green pastures" (2). Makes me? Why? Sometimes our minds go one hundred miles an hour and we don't know how to hit the brakes, slow down, and be still. Sometimes, we're just too busy being busy to recognize the need for rest, and at other times, we are so looking forward to upcoming possibilities and dreaming big dreams that we fail to be present and live in the moment—even as we forfeit opportunities for the sweet things of life. And sometimes, we go through the motions of withdrawal and solitude, but we are actually disengaged, empty. This is a form of spiritual escape, not rest.

I have come to believe that lying down in green pastures *is* a spiritual discipline. It is good for mind, body, and spirit. In this chapter, we will examine what it means to surrender, rest, and dwell in green pastures. Truly, we were made *for* rest, and if disregarded, we will be made *to* rest. It's as simple as that. We, all of us, need rest.

\*　\*　\*

## Rest

St. Jerome is credited as the author of this all too familiar saying: "Good, better, best. Never let it rest. Till the good is better and the better is best." Never let it rest, indeed. That's the mantra of our culture, isn't it—never let it rest, and never rest yourself? We are so intent on getting another blue ribbon, a promotion, a certificate of participation, or another line on our resumes, and not disappointing anyone on a local church committee or in our neighborhoods that we are always on the go, never making rest an integral part of our daily routine. Our culture celebrates the busy life, a one-activity-after-another lifestyle, as if it is normal and good. It isn't.

We know that rest and renewal, while not the same thing, are intimately related. According to the book of Genesis, God rested on the seventh day: "By the seventh day God had finished the work he had been doing; so on the seventh day he rested from all his work. Then God blessed the seventh day and made it holy, because on it he rested from all the work of creating that he had done" (2:2–3). When the work was finished, God rested rather than scurrying on to the next task or giving a state of the creation speech, even though there was much more to do. There's a lesson in this creation account for all of us. When we finish the work, it is time to rest and reflect. In fact, God blessed the seventh day and made it holy. Rest, it follows, is a holy activity.

We were made for rest, part of the natural rhythm of our days. We go, we do, we work, we play, and then we rest. Over my years as an academic dean, I've watched hundreds of college freshmen arrive on campus for the fall semester, full of energy, hopes, and dreams, but by mid-November they are worn down, worn out, exhausted, discouraged, and sick. Without the good judgment and discipline to include physical exercise, eating, and sleep as an integral part of their daily schedules, they threw themselves fully into the activity-rich, sleep-deprived campus scene, and ended up with a severe cold, mononucleosis, depression, or even worse. They were made for rest, but tried to postpone it till semester break. Many didn't make it, and they paid a real and substantial physical and emotional price for not doing so.

Most of us reading this book can smile a knowing smile at immature college freshmen who run themselves into the ground, but don't many of us do the same thing? We excuse our lack of good judgement and discipline regarding rest because our jobs demand it or our kids need us or we just like to be on the go. And as a result, we end up with a severe cold, mononucleosis, depression, or even worse. Too often, we commiserate that there's not enough time in the day to get everything done. Probably true, but some things can and will wait until tomorrow. When it comes to the choice between getting one more thing done and resting, please choose rest. The to-do list can wait, renewal can't.

We are made *for* rest, and many of us have learned the hard lesson that if we do not attend to this reality, we will be made *to* rest. We get the word from our doctor or physical therapist or spiritual director that we need to take time away, stay off our feet, and rest—and we need to do so now! And when we do, we find out that others will step in to fill the gaps in our jobs, our churches, and our families. We learn that we are not quite as indispensable and important as we thought or hoped we were. And we learn that it helps no one when we run until we are unable to show up.

I have come to believe that rest is critical, an important, restorative spiritual practice, every bit as important as prayer, work, study, and physical exercise—perhaps even more so because rest fuels all the other spiritual practices. When we are emotionally exhausted and physically ill, we lack the strength and resilience to pray, work, study, or exercise effectively, activities that will shape and form us in good ways. When we are weary, we simply don't have the stamina to lean into the things that will give us life, and shape our lives, too. Rest is a formative, life-giving spiritual practice—a holy practice. We were made for rest.

## Surrender

Rest comes in many forms. We can sleep in, go away for a long weekend, occupy ourselves in the kitchen or the woodshop, cancel some appointments, take the day off, or just veg on the couch—working the remote in search of something interesting to occupy our time and fill our day. Of course, there are many others, and it is fair to say that we all have our own individual approach to rest. We do it in our own unique way, but the writer of Psalm 23 is quite specific, "He makes me lie down . . ." (2). Not stand, not sit, not our way, but lie down. I think it is important to remember that David was a warrior, a fighter, a strong leader. I can just picture King David and his fighting force in the middle of the battle being led into a quiet, green pasture for some rest. OK, that's good. He would know from experience that even the strongest of his warriors needed some rest, even in the midst of the battle, but he also knew that you have to be on your guard because the enemy can show up at any time, unannounced. You have to be in control of the situation. So, no one sits or stands around. Yes, the fighters can rest a bit, but they must always be on guard, too, with one eye open and on the lookout for danger, ready to fight.

But wait, the order is not to simply rest, but to lie down. This is counterintuitive and confusing for someone in the midst of the battle, to be sure. This is not what a warrior was trained to do, even in green pastures, but it is apparently exactly what warriors (and worriers) need to do—to lie down, to be vulnerable, exposed, visible—to rest in God's care. When we are made to lie down, literally or spiritually, it is an act of surrender. We stop trying to be the leading hero, to win the battle all by ourselves, and we submit to God's wisdom and care. We yield to God's guidance and we relinquish control, one of the hardest things for a fighter to do. But when we do, it allows us to cease from striving to be right, wanting to be magnificent, needing to be the winner, and hoping to be perfect, and to just lie down and rest, fully depending on God for safety, rest, and renewal, even in the midst of our most difficult and desperate situations. To lie down takes courage, trust, and humility—all expressions of a deep faith in the good shepherd.

## In Green Pastures

What a pleasant thought—to lie down in green pastures. Yet in today's vernacular, the phrase "green pastures" often means "greener pastures," something new, better, bigger, or a more interesting place, job, or activity to pursue. And as we are often warned, the grass always looks greener on the other side of the fence, meaning that people are rarely satisfied with their own situation, thinking that others have it so much better. Of course, this is a myth. The grass isn't always greener on the other side of the fence. In fact, it rarely is, as many of us have learned the hard way. Why we overlook the negatives in other pastures and accentuate the shortcomings in our own is difficult to explain, but we do—all the time. Contentment, it seems to me, is an integral aspect of serenity, and it comes when we develop the ability to see things as they really are and accept them for what they really are. Such insights, I believe, are learned spiritual disciplines.

In a spiritual sense, green pastures symbolize God's care for us, the provision of spaces to not only take sustenance, but also to rest and enjoy tranquility, peace, and safety. The Christian life has two elements in it, the contemplative and the active, and often we think of a green pasture as a place to refuel after our activities and rest up from them, which it is, but it is more than that. It is also a place of meditation, reflection, and communion. Green pastures offer rich provision for both rest and spiritual renewal, where there is both delight and plenty.

But green pastures do not just appear ex nihilo. The shepherd prepares green pastures for the flock out of a dry and rugged terrain. Unwanted brush and bushes have to be removed, weeds have to be pulled, and stones carried away. Green pastures are the result of foresight, intention, and disciplined work. And so, when we are made to lie down in green pastures, in a spiritual sense we are accepting the care of the good shepherd who has prepared a place for each of us. Then it is up to us to take full advantage of the green pasture. Sometimes, this place is a secret garden or sanctuary that we return to time and time again. It may be a certain bench in the park, a chapel, a back-porch swing, or a room with a view, places where God feels especially close and intimate conversations abound. In the Celtic tradition, such places are called "thin places." There is an ancient Celtic saying that heaven and earth are only three feet apart, but in the thin places the distance between heaven and earth disappears altogether. There, one is able to receive a glimpse of the glory of God. I like that description very much. We all need to have thin places in our lives and take advantage of them every chance we get. Catching a glimpse of the glory of God will fill your cup.

However, we can't always sit and watch a Pacific sunset or take a walk through a redwood grove at dawn, as magnificent and life-giving as such activities can be. Happily, we can also find green pastures much closer to home. For instance, the local church has become a green pasture for me, a place of spiritual renewal. Since I began to think of church attendance and service as a spiritual practice rather than a pious and public duty, I have been shaped and formed in ways unimagined. As I have been challenged to lie down in this green pasture, I have received a multitude of blessings from the good shepherd—rest, renewal, delight, plenty, and fellowship, to name just a few.

Let me mention one other green pasture or thin place—the faithful fellowship of a few good friends, perhaps two or three persons who know you, love you, and talk with you honestly and candidly about spiritual things. They believe in you and expect nothing from you except your honest presence without masks or disguises. These are your people, the people with whom you can laugh, cry, doubt, and question as you journey home together. Such green pastures are hard to find and require care, but they are the stuff of the good life—thin places where heaven and earth become as one. To lie down in such pastures is never a chore but rather a gift, one that leaves you feeling closer to God and makes you a better neighbor.

## Be Thankful

In the epigraph of this chapter, Wordsworth succinctly interconnects rest and thanksgiving. I would be remiss if didn't do the same before we look at a passage from Scripture that highlights our need for rest and renewal, and the graceful provision of green pastures. Of course, it is good to give thanks when we are at rest, particularly so since we were physically and spiritually made for rest. Being grateful for opportunities to lie down in green pastures is the right place to start, but I think there is a more direct connection between rest and thanksgiving. When we lie down in green pastures, it provides an opportunity to reflect on God's goodness and generosity, to be thankful for the grace we have received in so many ways and at so many times in our journeys. Resting gives opportunity for heartfelt reflection and thanksgiving.

And would it be too much of a stretch to link rest and thanksgiving in yet a more direct way? When we are made to lie down in green pastures, surrendering to the overwhelming abundant supply of renewable spiritual resources that are all around us, it *is* an expression of gratitude, a spiritual practice of relinquishing control and accepting the care of the good shepherd, to be shaped and formed in gracious holy ways.

So, Wordsworth's encouragement to rest and be thankful makes divine sense. Far too often we take rest and renewal for granted. I love the prayers that begin by thanking God for blessings, known and unknown, remembered and forgotten. I have come to believe that being made to lie down in green pastures is a blessing that is often misunderstood, taken for granted, or forgotten. The grace and wisdom of the good shepherd at work in our lives is a spiritual gift, a blessing, providing rest, renewal, and the opportunity to express thankfulness—and to practice thanksgiving, too.

## Scripture

"Come to me, all you who are weary and burdened, and I will give you rest. Take my yoke upon you and learn from me, for I am gentle and humble in heart, and you will find rest for your souls. For my yoke is easy and my burden is light" (Matt 11:28–30). I am struck by the verbs found in this beautiful passage—come, take, and learn. They are compelling and inviting, reminding me of a set of spiritual practices for all of us when we seek rest and renewal.

Come. Come to the green pasture, and rest will be given to the weary and burdened, and that is certainly an apt description of our situation, isn't it? We are burdened by trying to do this spiritual life thing on our own and with our own strength and resolve, and we are wearied as a result. Rest is the gift of life and renewal that is offered, starting with one simple action on our part—showing up. I have come to believe that rest is a form of grace, something that cannot be earned or manufactured, but is offered to us freely and abundantly.

Take. This is receiving, accepting, and taking the yoke, one that was made for us and fits well, working in concert with God rather than trying to pull the load all by ourselves or go in another direction, which is so often our custom. It is intentionally aligning our actions and attitudes with the desires and direction of the good shepherd. It is allowing our internal spiritual compass to be shaped and formed, setting our direction to true north.

Learn. And as we align our behaviors and attitudes with the guidance and intentions of the good shepherd, we lie down in green pastures. We learn that partnering with God, receiving direction and care, *is* the way to grow and gain strength, purpose, and resolve. It is a needed lesson for all of us, and sometimes it takes longer than it should because we act as though we know more than the good shepherd, or we don't really need a shepherd in the first place—so we go our own way. Such attitudes and inclinations usually land us right in a thicket, far from the safety of green pastures, crying out for help. Why is it that we so often have to learn the hard way, from our mistakes, only to learn at the end of the day that God's yoke is easy and the burden is light? May we all have the courage and humility to come, take, and learn—to lie down in green pastures, resting body and soul.

## Some Practical Advice

Before we conclude this chapter and consider some questions for reflection and discussion, thoughtful practices that are often neglected and sorely needed, let me offer just a few words of practical advice.

### Establish a Healthy Rhythm in Your Life

First, it is important to establish a rhythm in your life—physically and spiritually, that combines regular times of action and contemplation and rest. This rhythm is critical, and we pay a dear price when we ignore it. For starters, get out your calendar and make some appointments with yourself, setting aside some specific times for rest and quiet reflection, and then be as diligent with keeping these spaces open as you would for a lunch reservation with the person you love most in this world. Set aside time for yourself. It will pay dividends.

### Find True North

Second, develop a sense of true north. It is easy to blindly race through our days and our weeks and not really have a sense of what is really important. From experience, I can tell you that almost all that is important comes down to relationships in one form or another. Who are your people who deeply know you and love you anyway? Take time to reflect on the grace that is in these relationships, and what you might do to not only grow as a result of these relationships, but also what you might do to deepen these relationships, seeing them as a far-too-rare form of grace. Cultivate honest and deep relationships. Rest in their care. If you are lucky, you'll have two or three who will walk with you, even in your darkest days, and you'll walk with them, too. And if you can't name anyone who fits that description in your life, it's time to reach out and go to work. All of this takes time and effort, but I can guarantee that there are many around you who are in the same boat. Take a risk. Reach out and connect.

### Don't Overlook Nearby Green Pastures

Third, when you think of green pastures, don't overlook the obvious. In addition to a few genuine friendships mentioned above, your local faith community is rich in resources and full of grace-filled opportunities to get involved, serve, and make a difference. And in doing so, you will learn much about God's faithfulness and find both rest and renewal as you journey together. Envision regular attendance and participation as a spiritual practice. If you do, you will be shaped in good ways. Over time, we are all shaped and formed by what we regularly practice.

### Be Thankful

Finally, take time to be thankful. I suggest that you end each day with someone you love, if possible, sharing where you saw God at work that day and listing three things for which you are thankful. Intentionally ending the day in gratitude is a good discipline that invites rest and a good night's sleep. And if you are alone at the end of the day, take time to journal or blog, intentionally recognizing the care of the good shepherd, who cares deeply for you.

## Conclusion

In this chapter, we explored what it means to be made to lie down in green pastures. We first recognized the truth that we are made *for* rest, and if we do not attend to this reality, we will be made *to* rest. Rest, as it turns out, is a valuable spiritual practice, supporting other practices such as prayer, study, work, physical exercise, and proper eating.

We then thought together about what it means—and what it requires of us—to lie down in green pastures, a bit counterintuitive in this fast-paced world we live in, especially for warriors and worriers. But the Christian life has both an active and a contemplative aspect, and both need to be nurtured. We named two rich elements of green pastures that can feed our weary souls and fill our spiritual cups—a small circle of close friends and a local faith community. Finally, we ended by acknowledging the truth found in the epigraph of this chapter—when we rest, we can be thankful. In fact, rest can be an expression of thanksgiving.

At the end of the day, the good shepherd, one who is humble and gentle of heart, has prepared green pastures for all of us, and beckons us to come and rest, even if we are weary and carry a heavy load—perhaps especially so. All we have to do is accept the grace that has been extended to us, no questions asked or explanations needed. Just rest and be thankful.

## Questions for Reflection and Discussion:

1. Is rest and renewal a part of your current rhythm of life? If so, how?
2. Can you think of a time when you were made to rest? What came of it?
3. How would you describe your thin places? What do you experience there?
4. What part do deep friendships play in your green pastures? How might you nurture these important relationships?
5. When you take time to express gratitude, what are the first three things that come to mind?

## Psalm 23

The LORD is my shepherd; I shall not want.

He makes me lie down in green pastures . . .

## CHAPTER 4

## *He Leads Me Beside Still Waters—Serenity*

> The final wisdom of life requires not the annulment of incongruity but the achievement of serenity within and above it.
>
> —REINHOLD NEIBUHR

### Introduction

### Small Town Theology

When I was a junior in high school, three friends and I decided to meet together for a short Bible study and prayer time each morning before classes commenced. One of my friend's father was the pastor of a church located immediately across the street from the high school, a perfect location for our budding Bible study and prayer ministry. It was designed to be short and sweet—a simple reflection on a Bible verse or two, and then a time of prayer before we headed across the street and into our day. It proved to be a surprising success, at least if numbers are any measure of that sort of thing. The first few meetings were attended by just the four of us, but a month or so later we had to move our gathering from a small downstairs classroom to the main sanctuary of the church to accommodate a crowd of well over sixty students. As it turned out, we had more students faithfully attending our Bible study than some churches in our town had on Sunday mornings. My guess is that the brevity of the meetings was a good deal of the appeal. We met regularly during school days for the next two years.

As I recall, we were not a very sophisticated theological lot, giving little thought about how our theology shaped how we read and explained certain texts or the prayers we prayed. I'm not sure we even understood how different our personal theologies were—Reformed, Wesleyan, Pentecostal, and Lutheran, and looking back, it is a wonder that the ship ever left port. We just wanted to come together, affirm that we loved God, and start each school day with an honest affirmation of our Christian faith and an earnest prayer. It seemed to strike a chord with our classmates, who showed up week after week.

Our theological differences didn't amount to much until one of our classmates was tragically killed one evening by a drunk driver. Such events, of course, are difficult to understand at any age, but we felt that some type of unified statement needed to be made, offering solace and providing some perspective for our teenage Bible study attendees who were all reeling from the news and trying desperately to make some spiritual sense of it all. As I recall, we couldn't agree on much of anything beyond the opening line of our joint statement: *We are truly saddened to learn of the loss of our dear classmate and grieve along with family and friends as we all struggle to make some sense of this terrible tragedy.*

The truth be told, we never did make any sense of that tragedy. Some wanted to simply affirm that God is in control and we aren't wise enough to understand all that is going on, so we are to just believe and hold on—what I have come to label the "grin and bear it" approach to difficulties. We don't and won't understand, so we just say that God is in control, come what may. That approach didn't sit well with the rest of us, especially me.

Others wanted to point out that God could have and certainly should have stepped in and intervened, but clearly didn't. As a result, we had every right to be angry, and, in fact, to wonder why we should believe in a God at all, especially one who is going to leave us at the mercy of a drunk driver, totally abandoning us to the vagaries of this world. It's what I call the "I guess we're on our own and I'm mad about it" approach to tragedy.

Another approach was to try to smooth over the pain and anguish of our loss and address our questions by offering some bromides: God was trying to get our attention, or God needed another star in his crown, or another angelic voice has been added to the heavenly choir. Of course, these proved to be terribly unhelpful, even patently silly in reflection.

Perhaps the most surprising and alarming perspective for me was the idea that for such a tragedy to take place, there must be some type of unconfessed sin involving the person or the family, and if someone would step forward and confess, perhaps God's anger would be satisfied, and judgment would pass. Honestly, I had never conceived of God as petty, angry, or vengeful, and to this day I reject such an understanding of God's character because I have always found God to be good, loving, caring, and kind.

My approach was to find some sort of middle way or *via media*, an idea that goes back at least as far as Aristotle, although I certainly was not drawing on any philosophical understanding during my high school years. I simply rejected the idea that God would just plan and carry out such a thing for some unknown reason. That seemed far too cold-blooded for the God I believed in. And I could not believe that God simply didn't care about any of us, that we were all just left to our own wits. That didn't make any sense either. Somehow, I had to believe that God was as grieved about this tragedy as we were, and that God was still with us, working to bring healing and hope in the midst of this terrible event. I believed this to be true, or hoped I believed this to be true, but in the face of real pain and loss, it was difficult to make any statement make sense.

In the end, of course, we didn't issue a simple statement because there were no simple answers to be given. All we could do was grieve along with the family and our friends, and push on as best we could together, hoping to achieve some serenity within and above the incongruity we faced (to paraphrase Reinhold Niebuhr).

In life, we face all sorts of difficult and unexplainable circumstances, yet I have come to believe that serenity is possible, although hard earned, even in the most painful and challenging times. In this chapter, we will examine what it means to be led beside still waters in the midst of the chaos that surrounds us and at times overwhelms us, using this word picture as a metaphor for serenity. As we will see, serenity is both a gift and an act of faith.

## Led Beside Still Waters

The metaphor of being led beside still waters is a twofold delight. First, there is the idea that we are led (beside still waters). We are not left to our own wits and blind luck to find still waters. We will be led there if we will follow the voice of the good shepherd. That's good news. And we are not coerced, not dragged, not compelled, not even obligated to go there or get there. It is a conscious choice that is ours to make, but if we do, we will find still waters. That's good news, too, a promise worth exploring and pondering at length, which we will do in Part 2—Guidance. Suffice it here to say that the good shepherd knows the difference between still and stagnant waters and is eager to lead the way to serene waters that bring rest and renewal, even life itself. Our job is to learn to follow.

And beside still waters (we are led). Still waters, particularly in early morning or late evening, come to life when the dancing light transforms the surface of the waters into a visual masterpiece, bringing a peculiar and inviting sense of calm and serenity. If you've ever had the opportunity to rest by still waters at first light or at sunset, you know what a profound experience it is to be still by still waters. It renews the soul.

Of course, there is something moving to be near a rushing mountain stream or to watch the ocean waves roll in at high tide, but it is still waters that provide a reflection of the world as it is, even of ourselves, not as we wish it to be or hope it would be—but as it truly is. Still waters are windows with clear, clean glass, offering a glimpse of reality crisp with color, precision, and wonder.

And as the old saying goes, still waters run deep. That is to say, the glassy surface looks serene, and it is, but something has to be going on underneath or still waters become stagnant and begin to stink. There is a huge difference between a farm pond and a spring-fed lake. As we think about serenity, we are after something deeper, too. We want more than just farm pond serenity—walking around with a placid, happy face that we put on when we appear in public. As we are led to still waters, we desire a serenity that is deep, and runs deep, too. As we shall see, serenity that runs deep is ultimately an act of faith, a gift to be received but requires some sincere spiritual work on our part. It rarely happens in an instant, but the good news is that the good shepherd will lead us to still waters that are deep and life-giving. That's a promise.

In the next section, we'll examine serenity, contemplating why this sense of peace is such a difficult and elusive state of being to achieve and maintain. We'll then clarify its definition, list several impediments to serenity, offer some helpful approaches and perspectives to consider, and discuss several realities to be faced as we, all of us, work to maintain a sense of peace and serenity even in the midst of our most difficult circumstances.

## Serenity

There is a traditional Episcopal prayer that begins, "I will try this day to live a simple, sincere, and serene life." I have always been captivated by this prayer of resolve to be offered each morning, so much so that I wrote a book about this spiritual commitment, a book titled *Morning Resolve: To Live a Simple, Sincere, and Serene Life*. As I wrote the book I became convinced, and I still believe today, that of the three life descriptors/intentions (simple, sincere, and serene), serenity is by far the most complex, perhaps the most mystical, and certainly the most difficult of the three to achieve and maintain. Let me explain how I came to this conclusion.

First, when I make a commitment to live a simple life, there are certain things that I can do that will immediately move me in that direction. For example, I can clean out my closet and make a run to Goodwill or the Salvation Army. Most of our closets are at least 50 percent overstocked, and for many of us it is closer to 75 percent. Just how many shoes does one need to store away, collecting dust as if it were money? And how about hats and coats? A quick count in my own closet yesterday came up with seven coats and fifteen hats. Seven and fifteen—really? We start to simplify when we clear out and give away the things that clutter our lives. And the same goes for our spiritual closets, too. We simplify our lives when that which has been hidden away in the dark is brought out to the light of day, and the skeletons, wounds, and failures that we hide and try to ignore are dealt with in a careful and conscientious manner. There is simplicity to be had in clean closets. And there are obvious ways that we can simplify our calendars and our finances, too. With wise counsel and diligent planning—and time—a simple life is achievable.

And when we set our sights on living a sincere life, we can easily look for service opportunities in our own local faith communities (I can't think of a single caring faith community that is without a real need for faithful volunteers), in our own neighborhoods, in the not-for-profit organizations in and around our local communities, and in organizations that serve wider relief and support ministries worldwide. I guarantee that if you earnestly pray for eyes to see and ears to hear opportunities for service as you go about your day, even the most ordinary of days, more ways to love your neighbor and make a difference in the lives of others will present themselves than you can shake a stick at; and with intentional service to and for others, a sincere life grows and blossoms.

Serenity, on the other hand, lacks any kind of short list of things to do in order to quickly achieve it. It requires a bit more interior work, perhaps a good deal more. It is not just about doing things like taking a nap each afternoon and sitting on a park bench each evening, as helpful and renewing as these activities can be. No, achieving a serene life is a spiritual process developed over time, and ultimately a gift of grace and an act of faith. It is a way of making your way in this world, and at the same time rising above it. As such, it can be very elusive, particularly so in our fast-paced, materialistic, media-driven, results-oriented world.

And I must confess that I am writing this chapter just back from a three-week retirement trip/celebration in Hawaii. Still, despite the serene surroundings, little worries kept tiptoeing in like ants at a picnic, even while I was at the beach at sunset counting sea turtles in the crashing, turquoise waves! Is serenity the complete and total absence of any worries? I hope not and do not think so. If it is, I'm afraid we would all be in trouble. I know I would. So, what is serenity, what are the major impediments that keep serenity at bay, and how might we live in such a way that we not only have serenity in the midst of our daily lives, but we are also led beside still waters with a deep peace and profound contentment even on our most difficult days, when we're in the ditch?

## *Defining Serenity*

*Serenity* is from the Latin word, *serenus*, plus the suffix *itas*. The first part of the word is the English adjective, serene, which means calm and peaceful. The Latin suffix corresponds to the English suffix -ity, and means "quality or state." When we think about serenity in this way, words such as composed, tranquil, still, untroubled, and clear and bright skies, come to mind—all signaling a sense of peace and calm. It is interesting to note, however, that the suffix, -ity, means quality or state of being. I like this extension of the meaning very much because to be composed, tranquil, and untroubled is, of course, a wonderful thing, but such feelings can be quite transient. However, having a sense of peace and calm that is an enduring quality or state of being suggests a certain longevity or permanence, a way of living, even in the midst of difficulties. Perhaps even more so in the face of our troubles in our darkest valleys.

In the Bible, *peace* is used in several different ways. It can simply mean freedom from strife or the absence of war, as in Joshua 9:15: "Then

Joshua made a treaty of *peace* with them to let them live, and the leaders of the assembly ratified it by oath." However, the same word is used to describe a spiritual assurance that God is present and cares for each of us: "And the *peace* of God, which transcends all understanding, will guard your hearts and minds in Christ Jesus" (Phil 4:7). When we are led beside still waters, it is this way of life or state of being that we desire, and in the last analysis, it comes as a gift of grace from the good shepherd.

## Impediments to Serenity

Surely, we all desire to be led by still waters, to live in such a way that peace and assurance abound. So why is it so difficult to do so? Even though serenity is ultimately a gift from God, it requires some work on our part. Spiritual growth is always a partnership, never a solo act. Far too often our own attitudes and behaviors get in the way. They become roadblocks and detours—impediments to serenity. Let's start by looking at what I call the Big Three Impediments to Serenity: refusing to let go, failing to move on, and struggling to start over. As you will see, these activities can become toxic, and when they do, they thwart our best intentions and work against our deepest desires for serenity.

Letting go can be hard, very hard, particularly when the letting go involves some of our most tender dreams, highest hopes, and best efforts. It is even harder when it comes to slights, hurts, and mistreatment we have received—things uninvited, unexpected, and largely undeserved. And letting go of a failure or a profound disappointment may be the hardest of all. If we are not careful, these events can easily and quickly lead to resentment and bitterness, and we tend to hold them closely and nurture them like a newborn baby. We join with the psalmist in praying: "But may you have mercy on me, LORD; raise me up, that I may repay them" (Ps 41:10). Repay them, indeed! I must admit that I have breathed such a prayer on an occasion or two myself, but it has never been helpful or edifying. Sadly, resentment and bitterness sour the spirit, and can easily become an impediment to serenity. Learning to let go can be a difficult spiritual discipline for many of us, but it is a major step toward still waters.

Dealing with the second of the Big Three is equally challenging: failing to move on. It is a close cousin to letting go. As we begin to let go of the bitterness and resentment that we carry, the next step is to move on.

Of course, this is easier said than done, but why is it easier for some than for others? I think it has a good deal to do with pride. Sometimes we just can't believe that something like this could happen to us, so we spend our emotional and spiritual energies trying to rationalize the outcome or blame someone for it, all the while feeling sorry for ourselves. Even when it is clearly the fault of others, it does little good to keep chewing on the same subject day after day. I have a good friend whose dream for his department was shot down unnecessarily and unkindly by the CEO. Even in his retirement, years later, he is still bitter about the CEO's actions, and he just can't let it go and move on. He is paralyzed by his wounded sense of pride, stuck in the mud, unhappy, and unable to move on to other avenues of productive service. Every lunch conversation goes back to this event and the resentment he carries. He will acknowledge that he needs to move on, but he never does. Honestly, it makes eating alone a welcome option. Moving on is a spiritual discipline, too, another step toward a serene way of life.

The third of the Big Three Impediments to Serenity involves the need to start over, something most of us have to do at one time or another during our lifetime—in relationships, in jobs, in careers, and in our hopes and dreams, too. For a few of us, starting over can be a new adventure and a fresh start; for most of us, it is hard work shaded by disappointment, not part of our original plans. Still, we lean in and do what we have to do to move on. Sadly, for some, however, starting over is an impediment to serenity because each day serves as a reminder of a past failure, bringing with it the terrible twins—guilt and shame. And often, feelings of being a failure show up, too. This toxic trio (guilt, shame, and a negative self-image) can pollute still waters, robbing both perspective and confidence, things that are needed for the spiritual journey ahead.

Surely, if we are to reside beside still waters and enjoy the serenity that such waters offer, we need to deal honestly and openly with the Big Three, but there are two other impediments that bear mentioning. The first is faulty theology. Simply put, it is terribly difficult, perhaps impossible, to make serenity a way of living if we conceive of a God who is angry, judgmental, vindictive, needy, and capricious. This is miles away from the Twenty-third Psalm, where God is pictured as a good shepherd, a gentle guide, and a gracious host. These metaphors invite a long stay by still waters and offer serenity to anyone who does.

Another impediment worth mentioning is complexity. This may sound rather vague, and in some ways it is. Here I am thinking about the ways that our lives are not only busy, but also increasingly complex. I have come to believe that being busy is not a bad thing, something to be managed by all of us and actually life-giving to many of us. Being busy does not necessarily rob us of serenity, but complexity is a dimension of life beyond busy. Life can become so convoluted, so challenging, so confusing that we find ourselves in an overwhelming state of anxiety, confusion, and bewilderment. Such disorientation is not the path to still waters. Earlier I suggested that there was a connection between living a simple life and finding serenity. This is what I had in mind. When we intentionally focus on simplicity in our lives, we work against the complexity that makes living a serene life so much more difficult, and sometimes impossible. Being busy is a season of life at one time or another for all of us, but being overwhelmed and disoriented robs us of our ability to find rest and renewal by still waters.

So, given all the impediments to finding serenity beside still waters, is it really an impossible task—just a pipe dream? The answer is "no" and that's good news. It is important to be aware of the impediments that can complicate our journey to still waters and to deal with them forthrightly, but there are also positive and productive steps that we can take as we follow the good shepherd. We'll look at several perspective and approaches for taking full advantage of still waters next.

### *Perspectives and Approaches to Serenity*

I can still hear my mother's words as I tearfully reported about accidentally breaking one of her flower vases: "There's no use crying over spilt milk." Of course, there is a good deal of wisdom in that statement. It is surely good to feel some remorse about breaking a valued item (and to express it) but worry and shame won't bring it back. No use crying over spilt milk; just lean in and help clean up the mess—and maybe think about how it could be replaced. After that, in my mother's wisdom, it's time to let it go. No obligation or condemnation. It is not insensitive to move on; it's healthy.

"It wasn't meant to be," is another of mother's sayings. Honestly, I didn't like hearing that one—thinking that it was the same as resignation to the inevitable, giving up. The older I get, however, the more the wisdom of her words speaks to me. Acceptance is not the same thing as resignation. Sometimes, things don't work out and I see (often by looking back) that they just weren't meant to be. Nobody's fault, nobody's failure—time to move on to still waters.

One saying that I've heard recently in an attempt to offer some peace to difficult and hurtful situations is this: "God is in control." I am not fond of this approach for three reasons: (1) such a stance lends itself to abject resignation, signaling a theology that there were no other possible outcomes; (2) it greatly diminishes our own efforts and agency in situations; and (3) it points the finger of blame at God for everything that happens. To me, this is simply not helpful in the face of tragedy, and it can lead to a sense of helplessness and hopelessness in life. If we are after still waters, it is far better to affirm that "Jesus is Lord." That keeps God in the ballgame and does not relegate us to a seat in the bleachers.

So, can these approaches to living really provide still waters? I believe they can. Remember, serenity is a spiritual discipline, an attitude, a way of being, and a way of making our way in the world. It is a perspective that while we do not control all that happens to us, we have a significant part to play, and how we respond to disappointments and difficulties, even those of our own making, matters greatly. Surely, developing such a perspective takes work—and time. It is a lifelong process, not a quick fix. It is the realization that acceptance is not resignation or laziness; there are things that are simply beyond our zone of control. And worry won't help. It is the assurance that living calmly and peacefully is possible, but we won't live it perfectly. After all, we are called to be faithful, not perfect. The key is to find still waters both within and above the events of our lives, a subject we will take up after we look at a particularly applicable story from the Old Testament.

## Scripture

"Forget the former things; do not dwell on the past. See, I am doing a new thing! Now it springs up; do you not perceive it? I am making a way in the wilderness and streams in the wasteland" (Isa 43:18–19). This is a profound promise, and one that I think we can appropriate and apply to what we face in our own daily lives. Part of the key to realizing serenity is selective memory—forgetting the former things and refusing to dwell on the past. Instead, focus on the new things that God is doing in your life, leading you to still waters, even to streams in the middle of a wasteland.

So, do not dwell on or get stuck in the past—that's good advice but that doesn't mean that the past should not be remembered. In fact, looking back is a powerful contributor to serenity. Remember when the children of Israel finally (after forty years) crossed the Jordan River and entered into the promised land? God instructed Joshua to have twelve stones (one representing each of the twelve tribes) to be carried from the river and made into a monument to mark the crossing, and they were to serve as a visible reminder of God faithfulness to future generations. In fact, when their children and grandchildren asked what the stones meant, they were instructed to tell them about how they crossed over the Jordan River on dry ground. They were stones of remembrance (Josh 4:1–9).

Certainly, there is a message here for all of us. Focus on the new thing that God is doing in your life, but also remember and reflect back on God's faithfulness. As it turns out, gratitude and serenity are closely related—as one looks back in gratitude, it gives peace and calm for what lies ahead, even if we do not know where we are headed—and that is most of us.

## Some Practical Advice

Before we close this chapter with some questions for reflection and discussion, I would like to offer all of us some words of practical advice for achieving a measure of serenity in the midst of difficult times while staying above them at the very same time. Serenity on two levels, if you will. That's the key. It takes practice, as do most spiritual disciplines, but it can be done!

### Acknowledge God's Presence

In the midst of difficult times, it is easy to feel terribly alone, and to be left alone, too. So, where is God when you find yourself in a dark place? He's right there with you, working to bring healing, hope, grace, and growth. Ignatian spirituality is grounded in the conviction that God is present and active in our world and in our lives. In fact, one Ignatian spiritual practice is to say to yourself anytime you face something difficult or uplifting or terrible or wonderful, which is every day, all the time, "God is present." Even in the middle of a terrible argument with a loved one or a horrible conversation with your boss, say to yourself, "God is present," over and over again. It may sound simple, but it is not simplistic. It can bring a profound sense of serenity in situations that we would all choose to avoid if we could. And by the way, repeating "God is present" brings a sense of serenity and gratitude in good times, too. Try it.

## Maintain Self-Care

There are many other resources and strategies that nurture a sense of peace and calm in difficult times, so let me name just three: self-care, relationships, and assistance. First, being aware of the need for and taking concrete steps to care for yourself in difficult times is important and necessary. Making time for adequate rest, healthy meals, exercise, solitude, and support are usually the first things to go by the wayside during difficult times, yet we know that these are the very things to bring renewal. Self-care is the foundation upon which serenity is sustained.

## Tend to Healthy Relationships

Relationships matter. Difficult times can be isolating at the very time when the support and wisdom of others is very much needed. Helping you sustain a sense of peace and calm in the midst of dark times is one of the most valuable gifts that a close friendship can provide. Ultimately, developing and sustaining serenity in difficult times is a communal act, not a solo venture.

## Ask for Help

Don't be afraid to ask for help. This seems so obvious, but for many of us, asking for help is really hard to do, and even harder to do when we need it the most. To look someone in the eyes and saying, "I need your help," takes courage and humility, but it will put you on the road to serenity. Self-care, relationships, and assistance—powerful strategies to sustain peace and calm in the midst of difficult, even terrible, times.

### Live Above the Fray

We have just been discussing some strategies for maintaining serenity in the midst of difficulties, but is there a way to maintain a serene perspective or way of life that carries you above the day-to-day difficulties? I believe that the answer is yes. We can have serenity in the midst of situations, while staying above them, too, maintaining a perspective that brings peace and calm.

Let me suggest three elements of an above-the-fray peace of mind and heart. The first is to recognize that serenity is a process, not a magic trick that can be conjured up with smoke and mirrors. It takes time-on-task, humility, and help, so don't be discouraged if serenity does not arrive in the first five minutes. It will come.

Second, it is essential to maintain a healthy perspective about the difficulties you face. Here are three serenity affirmations: this is only for a season, this is not life-threatening, and this doesn't define my entire life. I know these self-affirmations sound obvious, and in some ways they are, yet in difficult times, it is easy to slip into thinking that this *is* your entire life, that your life *is* ruined, and you will *never* recover from it. Honestly, these thoughts do come to all of us from time to time, but we don't have to believe everything we think. As the old Persian adage reminds us, "This too shall pass." Honestly, it will.

Finally, to have an above-the-fray perspective, it is important to recognize and affirm that there is goodness all around—friends, family, neighbors, colleagues, and your local faith community. There is no need to be afraid. You are not alone.

## Conclusion

At the end of the day, we long for serenity: a peace of mind, a way of living, a way of life—that provides calm and comfort not only in the midst of difficulties, but also offers a perspective and assurance that allows us to see beyond and rise above them. Ultimately, it is a gift from God, who leads us beside still waters. It is up to each of us to come and drink. We do so when we take time to *look back*—remembering past difficulties and promises kept; we *look around*—seeing mentors, models, friends, and community; and we *look ahead*—carrying God's promises with us: "His love endures forever" (Ps 136:1); "His compassions never fail. They are new every morning; great is your faithfulness" (Lam 3:22b–23); and

"As the mountains surround Jerusalem, so the Lord surrounds his people both now and forever" (Ps 125:2). Amen and amen.

## Questions for Reflection and Discussion:

1. What elements of self-care do you regularly practice, and what elements seem to slip away during difficult times?
2. Do you have two or three sustaining relationships that you can count on through thick and thin? Are you that kind of friend to others? Could you be?
3. Is it difficult for you to ask for help from others during difficulties? If so, why do you think this is so and what concrete steps could you take to ask for and accept help when needed?
4. When you face difficulties, which narrative(s) comes into play for you: this will define me as a failure, my entire life is ruined, or I will never recover from this? Are there others?
5. As you look back on your life, do you recognize times when God has been faithful to you? If so, what tangible reminders of those times could you identify and display as a remembrance?

## Psalm 23

The LORD is my shepherd; I shall not want.

He makes me lie down in green pastures; He leads me beside still waters. . . .

# CHAPTER 5

## *He Restores My Soul—Renewal*

> Where do we even start on the daily walk of restoration and awakening?
> We start where we are.
>
> —ANNE LAMOTT

### Introduction

Just four little words—"he restores my soul"—but one powerful affirmation—elusive, complex, and at times confusing, yet so full of hope, so full of life. As Anne Lamott poses it, "where do we even start" when we think about restoration and renewal? We could start with the placement of this affirmation, coming as an exclamation mark of sorts, bringing connection and closure to the family of images discussed in the first part of Psalm 23: the good shepherd's provision, abundance without want, rest in green pastures, and serenity beside still waters. In one sense, renewal can be understood as the outcome or cumulative impact of these rich blessings. It's the spiritual resources the good shepherd uses to restore our souls.

Of course, this immediately begs a host of other questions. How does the good shepherd restore our souls? Can restoration happen in different ways at different times on our spiritual journeys? What part do we play in the renewal of our own souls? Are there spiritual practices that contribute to renewal, and other practices and behaviors that deform our souls? For that matter, what do we mean by the *soul*? Honestly, I'm not sure that we will be able to resolve all these questions, but in this chapter,

I will try to reflect on as many of them as is workable and offer a way forward. First, however, a story.

## Revivals

During the 1950s and 60s, my home church faithfully scheduled a fall and spring revival each year, as did many churches during that time, and they were big events for us—drawing upwards to one hundred souls on some occasions, even some visitors from neighboring towns. As I think back, it could be that there just wasn't much else going on in our small town, which was true, but they were exciting occasions nonetheless. Our fall revival was scheduled right after bean and sugar beet harvests so our farm families could attend, and it was the biggest of the two annual revivals. We scheduled an evangelist from far away, far in advance, and marked our calendars to be sure that there would be no double-booking of events. The fall revival was top priority in our church—bigger than Easter.

The evangelist would arrive with whatever fanfare we could muster, and the revival usually commenced on a Sunday morning with special services each evening the following week. The teen group (all five of us) would place posters in the local stores and gas stations and hand out flyers to unsuspecting customers as they left the local bank. As I remember, there were three types of evangelists: the promoter, the teacher, and the role model. The church board always secured a well-known promoter for the fall event if possible. The promoter evangelist was flashy, outgoing, loud, confident, brash, and determined to whip our church into shape and turn it into the soul-saving station that it was destined to be. Using a combination of fear, guilt, exhortation, and enthusiastic singing, the evangelist would send us out to the highways and byways to bring in lost souls. It was impressed upon us all that there was very little time left for such activities, so we had better get going. And it was dangerous work, too. Who knew when someone might get hit by a train on the way to church? That event actually happened during a revival in Indiana some years back, according to the evangelist, and he shared all the details—more than once. Of course, we were motivated!

Unfortunately, there was only one highway running through our town and we weren't even sure that we had any byways, so the results, to say the least, were meager. We could never be counted on to make the top five revivals listed in our denomination's monthly magazine, based on the average number of seekers who came forward and made new commitments. Still, we all did what we could, and we religiously avoided all railroad crossings the rest of the week—just to be on the safe side.

Spring revivals were more of a local event, accompanied by lower expectations for evangelism. Often, we would invite a teaching pastor from our region to preach. He (and it was always a "he") would take a chapter of some book in the Bible and spend the week teaching us about the nuances of biblical exegesis. Admittedly, many of the nuances were lost on the congregation, but we were interested in learning more about the meaning of Scriptures in their original contexts and languages as long as the King James Version could be used as the final source for judgement. This was at the insistence of our elders who saw themselves as the guardians against any liberal influences.

My favorite revivals were led by what I call a role-model evangelist, usually an area pastor who, although lacking the flash of the promoter or the language fluency of the teacher, was simply a good and kind person who talked with us, not at us or above us, about becoming more like Jesus—loving God with everything we had and loving our neighbors in the same way. That kind of preaching really took with us and moved us, and the service would often end with the congregation gathered around the altar in the front of that little church, singing choruses about God's grace, peace, and love. The Spirit would break through, as we would describe it, and there wasn't a dry eye in the house. I'm sure we would all join with the writer of Psalm 23 and testify, "He restores my soul." That he did. We experienced renewal—deep, honest, and real. Memories of such times have shaped me even to this day.

* * *

As I think back, it seems to me that the fall revivals were focused on emotion, enthusiasm, and guilt. The evangelist worked feverishly to infuse new energy into the local congregation, trying to pump fresh air into an old tire. However, such an emphasis on emotions, on being "on fire all the time," had little lasting effect. The evangelist left and life returned to normal for the flock in about a week or so, sometimes sooner. After all, it was a small town and we all had to live there together. The old-fashioned tent meeting approach, full of fear, passion, and guilt, and separating the sheep from the goats by means of who made a trip to the altar, had outlived its usefulness and effectiveness.

The teaching revivals had more lasting impact. They provided the congregation with something to chew on, and although we were mostly common folk, we did think seriously about the Bible and how to live a godly and holy life. The teaching evangelist had the opportunity to shape our theology in helpful ways, seeing goodness and grace from a loving God at work in our daily lives.

I think the role-model evangelists had the most success because they walked their talk. Being local, they lived among us, and we knew them by the lives they lived before us and with us. Their sermons were powerful not because of their eloquence or learnedness, but because they were good people trying to love God and neighbor just like the rest of us. That stuck with us.

It seems to me that each generation and tradition has to re-embrace renewal in their own context and in their own words. For some, it will continue to be an emphasis on revival—rekindling and refreshing the emotions. For others, it will be more about right theology and effective teaching, a time for reframing the understanding of some key distinctives such as sanctification or the gifts of the spirit or evangelism. And still for others, the emphasis will be on spiritual practices that renew and restore faith and holy living.

At the end of the day, we, all of us, long for transformation, for a faith that carries us through our most difficult days and somehow transcends them, bringing hope and courage and perspective. And it is clear that we do not renew ourselves. Our souls are renewed by the good shepherd. In the next three sections, we will look first at the work of the good shepherd, then discuss several approaches to spiritual renewal, and finally examine what we mean by the soul. We will follow this up by looking for some guidance from Scripture and offering some practical advice before concluding with a few words of encouragement and promise for all of us who seek renewal in our own spiritual lives.

## He . . .

God not only works in mysterious ways, but in various ways, especially when it comes to spiritual renewal. Surely, renewal is a gift from the good shepherd, and it often comes to us quite unexpectedly. The lyrics of a song, the beauty of a poem, a memory, or a heartfelt blessing from a trusted friend can stir us in unforeseen ways, moving us closer to God. It changes not only how we see the world, but also how we make our way through the rest of the week. Certainly, we cherish these unforeseen comings.

Sometimes God visits us when we are gathered together in worship. In my childhood experience, we would say that the "the Spirit would break in" or "the Spirit came," and it did. The Spirit of love and comfort sought us out and came to us. It was real, and it couldn't be contrived or replicated because there was nothing we did to create it or deserve it. We didn't seek out those experiences; they just happened. I've watched many try to replicate or reconstruct such experiences, and they always come across as shallow and sometimes downright phony. Renewal is not a game of conjured emotions, but rather a blessing from the shepherd who cares for all of us.

At other times, renewal comes to us through a set of daily practices, the fruits of a long and faithful process. The rhythms, seasons, and intentions of our spiritual walk do shape and sustain our faith. Looking back, we see that the process itself was a gift that brought renewal.

Renewal can also come as the result of difficult times, being tested by fire, if you will. No one desires or seeks out such times, but they do come to all of us. And when we look back, we see the good shepherd's provision and guidance, and we realize that we have been changed for the good—renewed in spirit. We see the world differently.

So, there is no one prescribed or right way that God comes to us to renew our spirits. Even though most of us at one time or another have tried to bring on a spirit of renewal using a self-fashioned spiritual duck call, we soon learn that it doesn't work like that. This is God's work, not ours. He restores our souls in different ways at different times, and we are thankful for all the gifts that come our way—so unexpected, so undeserved, but so deeply appreciated.

## He Restores . . .

Of course, words like *restoration*, *revival*, and *renewal* can mean different things to each of us, so I think it is important to be clear about what we mean when we use these words. If not, it is so easy to say the same words and nod our heads in agreement, only to find out later that we had very different things in mind. Let me give just a short example. When I served as provost at Point Loma Nazarene University, the university's leadership team staged a "walkabout" just before students arrived in the fall. We would walk around campus and through each campus building, residence hall, and classroom, noting things that needed to be addressed or spruced up a bit. It was time well spent. When I arrived as provost at George Fox University, I heard the vice president of student life mention that the "walkabout" was scheduled for the following week. I immediately told him that I just loved walkabouts and wanted to participate. He had a strange look on his face and suggested that it wouldn't be necessary—he knew that I was busy preparing for my first year of service. I insisted that I would make time, and he tried again to dissuade me. I kept pressing the issue and couldn't understand why he was so reluctant to invite me to participate in such an important activity, until he told me that the GFU walkabout was an orientation program for student workers in the residential life unit, and they camped together and scaled one of the Three Sisters—a beautiful chain of mountains in central Oregon. Once I understood what he meant by the GFU walkabout, I was more than happy to stay behind and work on planning the faculty retreat! *Walkabout*—we used the same word, but it had a very different meaning for each of us. Clearly, we were not on the same page, and I almost ended up on an overnight camping and mountain climbing trip with students when what I really wanted was to walk around campus looking for things to be done before students arrived.

Unfortunately, the same type of misunderstanding can happen when someone insists that the church needs renewal or revival. Clearly, they have something specific in mind when they use words such as these and usually some specific ways for it to be achieved, but this may not be obvious to everyone else. In fact, the same words may have entirely different meanings, and this can lead to unnecessary disorientation and frustration on many levels—while planning the event, during the event, and even after the event when some type of assessment is conducted and discussed. Let's first define the word *restoration* (from *to restore*) and then discuss three words that are often associated with restoration: *revival, renewal,* and *renovation*. Hopefully, we can all get on the same page and avoid a few common misunderstandings.

To restore means to return something to a former owner, place, or condition. In a spiritual sense, I like the idea of returning our souls to a former owner, place, or condition—maybe all three. There are many synonyms for *restoration*, and that is certainly where some of the confusion lies. It can mean to repair, fix, mend, refurbish, recondition, rehabilitate, rebuild, reconstruct, overhaul, or redevelop. And there are at least three others that bear mentioning: revival, renewal, and renovation. Let's start with revival.

Revival, especially as portrayed on screens of all sizes, gets a bad rap, with scenes of guilt, fear, judgement, and emotionalism taking place in a big white tent with sawdust walkways. Many of us have experienced a few of these events ourselves, and very few of us want to return to those days when being faithful and spiritual had more to do with high emotions and fervor (being "on fire") than with right thinking or holy living. Revival had the implication that something alive had been lost or the holy fire had gone out, and more often than not, it was the loss of spiritual fervor that was the culprit, making us susceptible to works of evil of all kinds.

Unfortunately, it is not easy or healthy, in my view, to live in a constant state of heightened emotional enthusiasm—or fear. I honestly don't think that that is what God has in mind for us when the shepherd leads us to green pastures and still waters. Surely, to restore the soul means more than pumping air into leaking tires. It may serve you for a short trip, but the process must be repeated again and again and again if you are to get anywhere down the road in a spiritual sense. And with such an approach comes emotional fatigue and a spiritual walk constantly filled with peaks and valleys. This, to me, is not a prescription for restoration.

Renewal has a kinder, gentler, and less emotional feel for me. To renew means to take up again or resume after an interruption. It can also mean to reestablish a relationship or to reaffirm something as a priority. These actions of reconnection, taking next steps or reprioritizing one's life, have deep spiritual implications for us, and it is easier to see how one can go about this type of spiritual work, something we are doing together in this book. It seems to me that this is a more helpful approach to restoration, and certainly why more churches are providing both corporate and individual opportunities for spiritual renewal rather than focusing time, energy, and resources on periodic revivals. Renewal is an ongoing process using renewable resources, not an exhausting event held once or twice each year.

To renovate means to improve or redevelop something, usually through cleansings, repair, or rebuilding—making it new again. This may be an even deeper, complex, and more challenging spiritual process, one that calls for cleansing of the heart, repair of relationships, and rebuilding trust, confidence, and faith. It suggests a transformation, not just a fresh coat of paint. And I have come to believe that this transformational work is a corporate, not a solo, venture, requiring faithful friendships, wise counsel, and lots and lots of time and experience—not all of it necessarily welcome. However, spiritual renovation can transform us and enable us to transcend a daily spiritual struggle filled with fear, judgement, and feelings of abandonment and neglect.

I think this renovation of the soul takes time, and we don't always see the process at work. Usually, it is only when we stop and look back after particularly tough periods in our journeys that we can say with gratitude—made it! And from this perspective, we see that we have our spirits back and we are truly more humble persons. This type of restoration is honest, deep, and permanent, and our faith has been renewed. Indeed, the shepherd has restored our souls.

## He Restores My Soul

Before we end this meditation about the restoration of our souls, just a few words are in order about what the word *soul* suggests to me when I read this passage. First, let me be clear. This book was never intended to be a philosophical treatise on such concepts as restoration, spiritual renewal, or the soul, and clearly it is not. Nor is what follows an attempt at biblical exegesis or hermeneutics, as helpful as these disciplined efforts are for Christian thought and practice. Rather, I have been trying to draw my own insights and offer my own thoughts in an attempt to appropriate the text—that is, to explain what the text suggests to me and to propose what I think are some spiritual practices that we might take away and use to strengthen our spiritual journeys.

When I read that the good shepherd restores our souls, the first question that comes to mind is: what does a soul in need of restoration or transformation look like? I know that the vagaries of life and the banal voices of our culture can deform us and blunt our spirits. I once walked into the office of a colleague after a terrible meeting with my boss and exclaimed, "He broke my spirit!" What a sad comment to make, and a painful one, too. Something was broken. I was alive, but not at all well. I was a wounded soul in need of restoration.

The soul can refer to our life force, the breathing aspect of our being. We first read about God providing the breath of life in Genesis 2, and not only to humans but to animals of all kinds. And breathing and breath are mentioned in the Bible over 700 times, so it is certainly one prominent way to think about the soul. But soul can also refer to our spirit, the very spark of life. So, life force, breath, spark, and spirit all describe or represent some of what the soul entails.

Perhaps the best way to think about the soul is to acknowledge that it describes the entire essence of our lives—all of it, and different ways to see and express this essence take center stage at different times. Ultimately, I see the soul as the spiritual center that animates all aspects of our lives—mental, physical, emotional, relational, and spiritual. So, when we join the writer of the Twenty-third Psalm in exclaiming, "He restores my soul" (5), we are celebrating the embrace and recognizing the care of the good shepherd in all that we are and ever hope to be. He restores my soul. Just four little words—sometimes an event, often a process, always a gift.

## Scripture

### Peter's Failure

His spirit was broken, and he was embarrassed, too. After being one of the first disciples to join Jesus, then moving into the inner circle of followers, seeing miracle upon miracle, and making brash promises about his steadfast loyalty and unweaving commitment to the cause, even willing to face death, it all came crashing in one evening when he denied even knowing Jesus—not once, not twice, but three times—Peter failed to walk his talk, and after Jesus' death, he eventually made his way back to Galilee and did the only thing he really knew to do—grab his nets and go fishing. As we pick up the story told in John 21, Jesus meets Peter at the lakeshore the next morning, cooks him breakfast (so many remarkable spiritual events happen over a meal), and not only reaffirms his calling, but significantly expands it. Of course, Jesus had every right to shun Peter for his betrayal and kick him off the worship team, but instead he invited him into a deeper relationship and challenged him to feed his sheep—to be the rock upon which the church would be built. Jesus would not let Peter's ministry and influence be determined solely by his failures. Instead of casting him aside and making him invisible, he led him beside still waters and restored his soul. What a remarkable turn of events.

There is much to draw from this story of grace and restoration but let me mention just three. First, Peter failed miserably. We all do at one time or another. It did not mean the end of the line for Peter as far as Jesus was concerned, and it doesn't mean the end of the line for any of us either. In the midst of disappointment, shame, and outright failure, we just have to keep going and doing what we know to do, even if it is as mundane as going fishing or bringing the coffee for Sunday service. Keep leaning in, even when it is painfully embarrassing to do so. Restoration will come.

Second, Jesus came to Peter, not the other way around. When we fail and come up short, not living up to our own expectations and brash promises, our inclination is to retreat to a monastery or go on a six-month pilgrimage for renewal, trying to demonstrate our spirituality. For most of us, however, this just isn't possible, and the good news is that it is not necessary. After a colossal failure or a simple falling out, it is best to simply be present, to go about your business, whatever your business happens to be, and Jesus will come—and he will invite you into a deeper, intimate relationship.

Finally, restoration requires humility—to accept the grace that has been extended by God and others, and to forgive yourself. Jesus came to Peter, renewing and extending his call to ministry, but Peter had to accept this gift. Think of the consequences for all of us if Peter had refused to come to breakfast and accept forgiveness, rejecting an expanded call, and simply walked off down the shore. Every decision we make has its own moral trajectory, it takes you somewhere—and it impacts others, too. Having the humility and good sense to accept grace when it is offered is often the first step in renewal.

## Some Practical Advice

Before we conclude this chapter on renewal, let me offer a few words of practical advice.

### Clarify the Words

First, in any conversation about renewal, revival, or restoration, be sure to clarify what is meant by such longings or recollections. Is it the recovery of a feeling from the past or an opportunity to undergird a waning faith in God and the kingdom? Is it a desire for a more intimate relationship with

God or a deeper commitment to the work of the church? Is it a hunger to learn more about how to love God with everything you have and your neighbor as yourself? Is it a hope to revive a marriage or reestablish old friendships that have gone cold? Is it a longing for the restoration of your own soul or the renewal of the church? When you or someone else declares that the congregation *needs* revival, listen and ask good questions. Be sure that everyone is talking about the same thing. It is likely that they are not, and when this is the case, even well-meaning conversations and plans can lead to frustration and discouragement, even cynicism.

## Do Talk About What God is Doing

Second, it is certainly important to clarify the meaning of such terms as revival, renewal, and restoration, so do talk about them. These words carry deep meanings, longings, and possibilities for all of us, yet we often neglect to mention them at all, especially on Sunday. For some unexplained reason, we tend to hold such desires closely. So, speak boldly and often about what God has done and is doing in your life. It will certainly be helpful to others who are sensing the desire to grow spiritually but lack the language or experience to express it.

## Don't Try to Force Renewal

Third, remember that revival, renewal, and restoration are gifts from God, not some kind of magic trick that we can pull out to show off. Sometimes our souls are restored in totally unexpected and unimagined ways, and we are overwhelmed by and thankful for God's goodness to us. At other times, it is the culmination of long-standing, consistent, intentional spiritual practices that are blessed by God. In all cases, be sure to give credit where credit is due. Simply put, this is not our conjuring. In our daily spiritual walk, renewal may come to us as unexpected as a deer crossing our path, or in or as a result of tough times, or through our faithfulness to intentional spiritual practices. In any case, we give thanks; our souls have been renewed. Let God do the heavy lifting.

### Remember Why Renewal Comes

Finally, it is important to remember that our souls are restored for a purpose. Surely, we are restored when we lie down in green pastures and rest by still waters, but that's not where we live. Ultimately, restoration is about right relationships—with God, with our families, and with our neighbors. So, this means that we don't stay in seclusion at a mountaintop spiritual retreat or remain quiet about the work that God has done in our lives. At the end of the day, we return home—renewed, ready to love, ready to share, and ready to serve.

## Conclusion

He restores my soul—just four little words, but so packed with spiritual significance for all of us. In this chapter on restoration, we acknowledged that it is ultimately God's work—not ours. It can come to us in different way at different times for different reasons, and it can't be forced or contrived. Spiritual renewal simply doesn't work that way. Transformation is the province of the good shepherd.

We looked at the restoration of Peter after his now-famous denial and noted: (1) Jesus didn't let Peter's failure stand in the way of a relationship with him; (2) Jesus came to Peter, not the other way around; and (3) Jesus offered a meal and called Peter to an even deeper relationship and mission, something that Peter embraced with humility and thanksgiving. There is a lesson here for all of us.

And we closed with several words of practical advice: be sure that everyone understands the meaning of words such as revival and renovation in the same way to avoid confusion, but do speak of the restoration of your spirit—something we often neglect to share. Remember that restoration is a gift from God, not an action we do to try to please God; and be mindful that we are restored on purpose for a purpose—to return home ready to serve, share, and love.

Ultimately, restoration is the culmination of the many provisions of the good shepherd—who makes us lie down in green pastures and leads us beside still waters, and it can start with a simple meal. Indeed, he restores our souls.

## Questions for Reflection and Discussion:

1. Do you have any memories of revivals? Are the memories positive or negative? Explain.
2. Which word has more spiritual meaning to you—*revival, renewal,* or *restoration*? Why?
3. Where do you find yourself in the story of Peter's restoration and transformation?
4. We all come up short from time to time, and perhaps the hardest thing to do is to accept grace when it is offered by God or others. Are you able to let go of the past and embrace the gift of grace and renewal?
5. Is God calling you to a deeper spiritual walk—to transformation? How might you identify and embrace this invitation?

## Psalm 23

The LORD is my shepherd; I shall not want.

He makes me lie down in green pastures; He leads me beside still waters.

He restores my soul . . .

# PART II

# The Gentle Guide

He leads me in paths of righteousness for His name's sake. Even though I walk through the valley of the shadow of death, I will fear no evil; for You are with me; Your rod and Your staff, they comfort me.

—PSALM 23:3B-4

IN PART I, WE examined several metaphors related to the work of the good shepherd—green pastures, still waters, and the restoration of the soul. We noted that protection, plenty, rest, and serenity are gifts, grace itself, that culminate in the renewal of our spirit. It is God's work, not ours, and for that we are so thankful.

In Part II, we will look at another metaphor from Psalm 23—the gentle guide, and we will meditate together on the provision of companionship and correction for our journeys, even in our darkest valleys. And we will take courage that the gentle guide is always with us, whether we turn to the right or the left, even when we don't know exactly where we are going. God's voice encourages us and shows us the way home. Even when we require and receive correction from the rod and staff, our guide is gentle with us. For that, we are thankful, too.

So, we begin. We will examine the following ideas together: guidance (chapter 6), journey (chapter 7), courage (chapter 8), companionship (chapter 9), and contentment (chapter 10). We join with the writer of Psalm 23, taking heart that the good shepherd is also such a gentle guide. In Part III, we will find yet another framing metaphor, the gracious host, but let's not get ahead of ourselves. Suffice it to say here, one of the primary reasons that the Twenty-third Psalm is so endearing and has been so across the ages is because the writer has found God to be good, gentle, and gracious—all the time. Now that is a grace-filled trio! Let's focus now on the gentle guidance that is extended to all of us.

# CHAPTER 6

## *He Leads Me in Paths of Righteousness for His Name's Sake—Guidance*

> Slippings and strayings there will be, no doubt, but the everlasting arms are beneath us; we shall be caught, rescued, restored. This is God's promise; this is how good he is.
>
> —J. I. PACKER

### Introduction

When I think about God's guidance, it is at the same time both deeply assuring and honestly confusing. It is assuring because the idea of being left completely on my own, depending on my own wisdom and wits, or being led astray by someone or something or some idea is truly daunting and easily imagined. Quite frankly, I will take all the guidance I can get, especially from a trusted source. However, I must confess that I don't fully understand how God's guidance works or when it shows up or what it requires me to do. And to complicate matters, the Christian community has so many versions and methods for seeking and finding guidance that it makes my head swim.

In this chapter, we will examine what it means to be led along paths of righteousness for his name's sake, even when we slip and stray. We will look about some of the confusion that accompanies the idea of God's perfect plan for our lives and how we might think about God's guidance in fresh ways, and we'll examine what it means when we hear nothing at all from God, seemingly left to our own wits and worries. Then, we'll consider what it means to represent the family of God for his name's sake. Hopefully, along the way we'll be able to embrace the assurance of God's guidance and eliminate some of the accompanying fear and confusion.

## Five Guidance Vignettes

To frame our discussion, here are five vignettes about seeking and receiving guidance of one kind or another that come from my own journey. In sharing these short stories, I hope that we can all identify with one or two of them—and some of us with all of them.

### Vignette One: Direct Guidance

In the spring of my second year in community college, I agreed to accompany my mother to our Wednesday evening prayer meetings. Honestly, I didn't necessarily want to go, but I didn't want my mom to go alone either, so I drove her to our church. One evening as I sat in the back pew, I noticed a denominational newsletter in the hymnal rack, and since I wasn't paying much attention to what was going on around me, I grabbed the newsletter and began perusing its contents. I noticed a story about our denominational university, profiling some of the season highlights of the basketball team. At the time, I was considering a basketball scholarship offer from a major state university, but I distinctly heard a voice say to me, "You need to go there. It will be good for you." Honestly, I don't know if it was an audible voice or a voice speaking deep within my spirit, but I do know that it was real. It was direct guidance and I listened. I contacted the basketball coach, arranged a campus visit the following week, and transferred the following fall. Certainly, it changed the trajectory of my life. It *was* good for me, and I have never looked back with regret.

### Vignette Two: Abundant Guidance

As college graduation approached, I was considering what to do next. I had a generous scholarship offer to attend a graduate school of psychology, an opportunity to go to work with a promising, local startup company, and an invitation from our denominational seminary in Kansas City for study in the MDiv program. They were all attractive opportunities, and I just couldn't make up my mind. I made a long list of the comparative advantages and disadvantages of each one, and I prayed fervently and waited for God's direction. It didn't come. There was no clear indication as to what God wanted me to do. His still small voice was silent.

I scheduled a meeting with my faculty advisor, a wise and deeply spiritual person, and asked for his counsel. He studied my long and detailed analysis lists and listened as I recounted my many frantic prayers for guidance, then gently put his hand on my shoulder and asked, "What would you choose if it were up to you?" "Oh," I responded quickly, "I would go to Kansas City in a heartbeat." "OK, then, go to Kansas City," he said with a smile. "You can do that?" I stammered. "You can just make your choice even before God has directly told you what to do?" "Why not?" was the answer. "They are all great opportunities and God will be with you regardless of your decision. Since you don't feel a particular spiritual nudge or leaning for any one of them over the others, God in his abundance is giving you the choice. What a remarkable blessing it is to have choices."

And so it was. I headed for Kansas City, and I have never looked back with regret.

### *Vignette Three: Open Door Guidance*

In the fifteen years since my decision to head to Kansas City, I found my way into a career in Christian higher education—or, more accurately, it found me. I was attracted by a job posting for the vice president for academic affairs position at a prominent Christian university. However, I didn't know anyone at the university, and I was not from their sponsoring denomination, so I knew that my application had little chance of being seriously received and considered. Imagine my surprise when the president of the university called one evening out of the blue. We had a far-ranging conversation as he told me about the university and the open position, and I did my best to tell him about all my hopes, dreams, abilities, and accomplishments—things I thought would make me a stronger candidate. As I hung up the phone, however, I immediately felt that I had tried way too hard to "sell' myself and must have come across as a brash, inexperienced, overeager applicant. I just knew that this venture was over.

Imagine my surprise when a few days later I received an invitation to visit campus for a one-hour, face-to-face interview with the search committee. I was excited about this interview until I learned that I was one of eight semifinalists, and the only one without deep connections to the university—and most were local. I flew in and had a good interview, but I felt that that would be the end of the line for me.

Imagine my surprise yet again when I received word that I was one of two finalists, and I was to come again to campus, this time for a three-day interview. I studied and prepared as best I could and had three wonderful days of interviews on campus. I was growing to love the university very much. While there, however, I was told that the other candidate had deep connections to the university and the sponsoring denomination and seasoned experience in higher education, so my candidacy was probably too big of a risk for many on the search committee. I fully understood and left thankful for their gracious hospitality, appreciating the opportunity to learn during the interview process and ready to congratulate the other finalist, knowing full well what a wonderful job it would have been to work at that institution and with that president.

Imagine my surprise when the president called me a week later and offered me the job! I accepted the job on the spot. "Oh, don't you want a few days to pray and seek God's direction?" he asked. "No, not really," I replied, "the entire process was bathed in prayer and full of open doors. None of them closed, so I'm ready to come." I did, and it was good.

### *Vignette Four: Closed Door Guidance*

Later in my career, my wife and I were praying for God's direction about a possible career move. During a very emotional chapel service, I distinctly felt God telling me that it was time to go. I returned to my office only to find three phone messages from three different professional recruiters, each wanting to know if I would consider interviewing with them about an open university presidency. Wow! God works fast, I thought. However, each opportunity turned out to be a dead end, and personally painful, too. I ended the process a bit confused, humbled, and emotionally banged up. Still, I am grateful. Looking back, none of these universities would have been a good fit for me—or me for them. I was guided by closed doors, and it was good—although it took some time to come to that realization. Many things make more sense in the rear-view mirror.

### Vignette Five: Silent Guidance

The four vignettes above make me out to be quite a spiritual person—close to God, and hopefully I am, at least most of the time—but I must confess that God and I haven't always been on good speaking terms. That is to say, there have been times, more than once, in fact, when I have intentionally and ardently sought God's direction and guidance for important decisions, but I heard nothing, received nothing, and felt nothing—nothing at all. Honestly, I didn't know what to make of these times. There was no direct voice or discernible plan, no abundance of choices, no series of open doors, not even a closed door—just silence. I knocked and knocked at the door I encountered, but no one answered.

So, is it possible to be guided by silence? Can the lack of any serious inclination about what to do or where to go be a form of guidance? I have come to believe that it can be. When we feel lost, alone, and without direction, perhaps the best thing to do is to stay put or stay the present course until some kind of direction is perceived or until some doors open and others close. Sometimes, the message of silence is *not now, not yet,* or *it won't happen.* Sometimes the message of silence is *be still—wait, watch, and listen.* I have found that such silence is only for a season. In due time (but not usually on my desired timetable), God's guidance will become evident. Sometimes it will come in remarkable and unexpected ways like a voice in the middle of the night. At other times, God's guidance will come through the faithful and loving care of others or as a result of intentional, persistent spiritual practices. Truly, God does work in mysterious ways, but God also guides us through the ordinary events, activities, and relationships of our lives. In the end, it is all grace, and for all types of guidance, we are grateful.

*　*　*

In what follows, we will look at some conceptions and misconceptions about God's guidance in our lives (Paths of Righteousness) before considering what it means to remember where we came from and to whom we belong (For His Name's Sake). Hopefully, we will begin to see God's fingerprints all over our lives, in ways known and unknown, remembered and forgotten. Truly, we have been caught, rescued, and restored, to paraphrase the epigraph at the beginning of this chapter. Thanks be to God.

## Paths of Righteousness

Let's tackle the first word straightaway—*paths*. Notice that it is plural—paths, not path. I think this is significant when we reflect on God's spiritual guidance in our lives. I am aware that some Christians believe that God has a perfect plan for them, and to misstep is to settle for second best or lose one's way altogether. Of course, a perfect plan for each of us is inviting, to think that we are personally selected and set aside to walk a predetermined path that will lead to happiness and spiritual contentment. Sometimes I wish it were so myself, but I don't believe it is. I don't believe that God identifies a select few, ushering them through life like robots, blessing them if they stay on the path and punishing them when they miss a signpost or make a mistake. What would be the point? The *whoever* in John 3:16 is compelling; to me it means *any person—anyone*, not a select few or a private club.

And I know that Jeremiah 29:11 is a life-verse for many: "'For I know the plans I have for you,' declares the Lord, 'plans to prosper you and not to harm you, plans to give you hope and a future.'" Some scholars argue that this message was for the exiles in Babylon, not for any of us today. Therefore, to take such a verse as a personal promise in the twenty-first century is to read more into the passage than was ever intended. Other scholars disagree and argue that the promise of a hope and a future is an indication of the goodness and grace of God, and it is for everyone. There is neither time nor space here to enter in or attempt to settle such a long-standing debate, but I will simply point out, regardless of how you appropriate this verse for your own life, the operative word is *plans*, not *plan*—for I know that *plans* I have for you . . .

I believe that the plurals in Psalm 23: 3 (paths) and Jeremiah 29:11 (plans) are not accidental, and this is certainly supported by the prophet Isaiah, who wrote: "Whether you turn to the right or to the left, your ears will hear a voice behind you, saying, 'This is the way; walk in it'" (Isa 30:21). *Whether* you turn to the left or the right, either way, the guiding voice of God will be with you. To me this is encouraging news. My spiritual assignment is to love God and neighbor with everything I have, not to tiptoe around—hoping to stay on the right path and receiving the consequences if I don't. Clearly, we are not just left to make our own way in this world. There are righteous paths to follow. Micah 6:8 tells us that we are to walk on paths of justice, mercy, and humility. God's still small voice will guide us, but we are called to do our part, too.

So, what part do we play? First, it is important to expect that God will guide us. Such expectations will improve our spiritual sight and insight. Second, as the five guidance vignettes illustrate, guidance comes in many forms. Don't limit the wisdom of God by seeing guidance as coming to you in certain preordained or foreseeable ways. And third, be prepared to follow God's leading when it presents itself, regardless of how or when or why it comes your way. As my father was fond of saying, "No use asking for advice if you already know what you're going to do." I think the same holds true for God's guidance. We need to expect it, look for it, and follow it when it comes—and be grateful.

Yes, be grateful regardless of the outcome. Guidance requires us to act, but it does not insure success, particularly as success is defined in our culture. Simply put, there is no spiritual guidance insurance policy that provides universal protection from the vagaries of life. And at times, we will stumble and stray, but even our failures can be a form of guidance. That is, we can certainly learn from them and grow spiritually as a result. It is important to remember that our failures do not define us, but they can shape us in good ways. We are God's beloved, and we are not only guided in paths of righteousness for his name's sake, we are also guided in the sense that God is with us, whether we turn to the right or the left. God is committed to us and will lead us safely home. We are not called to be perfect, but to be faithful, and God will be faithful, too.

## For His Name's Sake

We are led in paths of righteousness for his name's sake, the psalmist tells us (23:3). For his name's sake—for the sake of the family name. In fact, for the sake of the family, our family. When my father dropped me off at college for my freshman year, he looked me squarely in the eyes and said, "Don't forget where you came from, son." It was a reminder that I represented more than just myself at school—I represented my family, too, and that meant that I was expected to conduct myself in a way that would honor the way I was brought up. I carried the family name with me wherever I went.

When we were married, my wife, Lori, had flowers placed on two empty chairs in the front row to honor her parents who were deceased. It was a way of remembering them for all they did to raise and support a young girl, and a way of honoring that what they believed was important in life. And at her graduation from seminary, Lori pinned pictures of her parents inside her gown as a way of saying that they were a big part of that accomplishment, and they were still with her in deep and significant ways. She remembered where she came from.

We all carry a family name in one sense or another, and we walk in paths of righteousness because this honors our spiritual family. We live faithfully and rightly because this is what is expected by our family and from our family—to walk in paths of righteousness for his name's sake.

## Scripture

I am always a bit skeptical when someone strings together a series of verses to support a predetermined point of view, a practice known as proof texting. Of course, it is not wrong to consult or quote Scripture for there is much wisdom to be mined there, but it must be done with care and always in context. In what follows, I will focus on six passages from Proverbs, Leviticus, and the Psalms to highlight the importance of discernment in our spiritual journeys. I do not believe that I am proof texting in this instance, but rather drawing from the wisdom that resides therein for all of us. However, that will be for you to decide, so discern carefully—which is precisely the point of this entire section.

### Discernment in Scripture

"In their hearts humans plan their course, but the Lord establishes their steps," Proverbs 16:9 tells us. This affirmation, it seems to me, highlights the fact that our spiritual journeys are a partnership, always in relationship. The Lord establishes our steps even as we plan our course. We are led in paths of righteousness for his name's sake, but we are not robots. There is a moral structure that guides our lives and there are opportunities for loving God and neighbor—matters of right and wrong, good and bad, kindness and compassion, grace and generosity, and when we ignore them our lives are diminished.

But we have an important part to play in this relationship. We are to listen for the voice of the gentle guide, learn to trust that voice, and act wisely. Proverbs 1:5 puts it this way, "Let the wise listen and add to their learning, and let the discerning get guidance." That's good advice for all of us.

However, learning to recognize and follow the voice of the gentle guide is often a daunting task because there are so many voices willing to offer unsolicited advice—the "you-know-what-you-should-do" folk. Be very careful. And "do not turn to mediums or seek out spiritualists," Moses told his flock centuries ago (Lev 19:31). I personally believe that this advice holds true for all of us. Be careful who you allow to speak into your life, but that doesn't mean that you should go it alone. Of course, your own intuition can be a very good source of guidance, but "the wise listen to advice" (Prov 12:15), especially from trusted friends, mentors, and spiritual directors.

Psalm 32:8 gives some valuable insight into God's guidance process and how it comes to us: "I will instruct you and teach you in the way you should go; I will counsel you with my loving eye on you." Here we see three processes at work, each adding an element of guidance. First, there is instruction of various kinds that leads to knowledge; then counsel from the still small voice, Scripture, close friends, and trusted mentors and directors that offers wisdom; and most importantly, the watchful loving eye of the Lord who knows us and desires the best for us. Discernment and guidance are ultimately about right and honest relationships—with God, with those we love, with our neighbors, and with ourselves.

Discerning guidance can be confusing at times, and we are often our own worst enemy. Our egos get in the way, and we lose our way—we stumble, but that doesn't mean that we are lost or we will have to settle for God's second best, if we can get home at all. No, "the Lord makes firm the steps of the one who delights in him; though he may stumble, he will not fall, for the Lord upholds him with his hand" (Ps 37:23–24). What a wonderful promise. The gentle guide delights in us, and we are upheld even when we stumble and lose our way. We are to learn, seek counsel, watch, and listen for guidance, and the promise is that direction will be given in the context of the many relationships we have, and we'll follow it and make our way home. Guidance, it turns out, is a team sport—not a lonely marathon.

## Some Practical Advice

Before we conclude this meditation on guidance, I want to offer all of us who seek spiritual guidance some words of practical advice. Hopefully, this will provide some tangible paths to follow as we journey home.

## Love What You Love

Many of us have heard stories about someone who wanted to be a doctor or lawyer or . . . but when they became a Christian, God called them to be a missionary to Africa instead, dashing their dreams but giving them a new heart and a new challenge. Now, I have no doubt that such life-changing events occur from time to time, but I think it is far more likely that your God-given loves are there for a purpose, and you should pursue them. That is to say, carefully assess what it is that you love, where your passions take you—and go there. Love what you love! They are there on purpose for a purpose. If you want to discern the Lord's leading in paths of righteousness, don't neglect your loves and passions.

## Listen for the Still Small Voices

Let me just point out two still, small voices that provide direction as we make our way in this world. The first is the whispering of the Holy Spirit—that still small voice that comes to us in the middle of the night or on a long walk, whether it is audible or lodged deep within your spirit. This voice is to be welcomed and followed. Honestly, I do not hear this voice as often as I would like, but it does come. And when it does, I am thankful and obedient.

The other still small voice is our own intuition, our ability to understand something immediately without the need for conscious reasoning. Some call it a "gut feeling" or a "red flag," the ability to read persons or situations without the assistance of a good deal of observation or time. I have come to believe that our intuitions are a form of discernment and guidance, so don't neglect them. Whenever you can, however, give your intuitions a double-check. That is, share your inclinations or concerns with a trusted friend or mentor to be sure that you are tracking accurately. It is possible to be mistaken about people and situations.

## Cultivate Relationships

Relationships come in all shapes and sizes, but most of us have one or two, or, if lucky, three relationships that are special. We are deeply connected with these friends, having shared our hopes, dreams, fears, and flaws with them—and they love us anyway. They love us so much, in fact, that they will tell us what we need to hear rather than what we would like to hear. These are true friends and a genuine source of spiritual guidance. Cultivate and care for these friendships as if the truth depended on it. In many cases, it does.

In addition to intimate friendships, there are two others that bear mentioning: mentors and directors. These are not personal friendships, but they are true friends in that they help us process thoughts, feelings, and opportunities with care and realism—pushing us to think about what God is saying or teaching us. These relationships are invaluable when trying to gain direction about a career move, a relationship, or an opportunity for ministry, to name just a few. Supportive and honest relationships are a gift. Cultivate as many as you can, and be this kind of person to others, too.

## When You See a Door—Knock

While serving as an academic dean over the years, I have had dozens of faculty members and professional staff come to me and share that they were particularly attracted to a job posting—sometimes within the university and sometimes somewhere else. I always give the same advice: "that sounds good—lean in and start the application process because you won't ever get that job if you don't apply. If you see a door, step up and knock." Now, I then hasten to add that the entire application process is really a dual-discernment process, for you and for your potential new employer. Along the way, such experiences teach us a good deal about ourselves, and it might lead to new opportunities for growth and development.

On the other hand, it might not. The door may close and all you have for your efforts are disappointment and frustration That's OK, too. As we look back, we all realize that we are shaped and formed more by our disappointments and failures than by our successes. It's not a happy fact, but it is true nonetheless.

And even if you get a job offer, you might feel led to decline it. If so, it often brings more contentment to your current situation, knowing full well that you could be somewhere else but chose to stay. In any case, when you see a door, give it a knock and lean in. Trust the process, seeing it as a discernment process not only for that employment opportunity but for your spiritual journey, too, whether the door opens, slams shut in your face, or is never answered. The discernment process itself is the teacher far more than the outcome.

## Conclusion

In this chapter, the first of five meditations exploring the metaphor of the gentle guide, five guidance vignettes offered a view into ways that guidance comes to us—as an audible voice, by an abundance of opportunities, through open doors and closed doors, and even in silence. We then discussed the importance of noticing that *paths* in Psalm 23:3 and *plans* in Jeremiah 29:11 are plural, not singular words, and noted the difficulties and restrictive theologies that can emerge when they are taken as The Path and The Plan. We noted that we are led in paths of righteousness *for His name's sake*—for the sake of the family, the name we carry with us, and that there are moral expectations for family members to act with justice, mercy, and humility even as we make our own way home.

We consulted Scripture passages from Proverbs, Psalms, and Leviticus that emphasized the importance of seeking guidance from a variety of sources including our own intuition and trusted friends before offering several words of practical advice: love what you love, listen for the still small voice, cultivate relationships, and knock on the door when you see one.

At the end of the day, we know that God's guidance comes to us in a variety of ways, and sometimes such guidance is abundantly clear to us and sometimes we are not even sure if God is speaking to us or present at all. And if we are honest, we acknowledge that sometimes we know exactly what path to walk and we choose another. Our own selfish desires and pride get in the way. Still, we take heart that we are called to be faithful (and repentant), not perfect. God's voice will be with us, whether we turn to the right or the left, and God will see us home—because this is how good he is.

## Questions for Reflection and Discussion:

1. Can you share a time when you clearly heard God's voice? Where did this direction lead?

2. Think of a time when you clearly heard God's guidance through a trusted friend, mentor, or spiritual director. Where did this direction lead?

3. Can you think of a time when you urgently sought God's leading, but there was nothing but silence—no direction at all? What did you do, and how did this experience impact your faith?

4. Do the plurals *paths* and *plans* in Psalms 23:3 and Jeremiah 29:11 change your reading of these passages and the implications for your own process of discernment? How so?

5. How might you offer guidance to someone close to you without becoming the "do you know what you should do" or "if I were you" kind of friend? How might you develop such trusted friendships in your own life?

## Psalm 23

The LORD is my shepherd; I shall not want.

He makes me lie down in green pastures; He leads me beside still waters.

He restores my soul; He leads me in paths of righteousness for His name's sake. . . .

# CHAPTER 7

## *Even Though I Walk Through the Valley of the Shadow of Death—Journey*

Not all those who wander are lost.

—J. R. R. TOLKIEN

### Introduction

We live our lives in a deep-seated tension between the longing to be at home or to establish one, and the desire to travel, to be on the journey. In one way or another, we, all of us, must negotiate this tension that compels us to leave home and to find it again—literally, figuratively, and spiritually. In chapter 15, we will examine the meaning of finding home and dwelling there in some detail, so we won't deal with this idea in depth here. Suffice it to say that making a home, finding a home, and going home are universal spiritual challenges for us all.

And at the same time, we are a bit antsy when we are at home, even in the most supportive and comfortable situations. We look to the horizon and wonder if we have missed an opportunity or two, and what might be waiting for us just over the next hill. We were made for home and for the journey, and we carry both yearnings deep within us. They are there, even though at most times they go unnoticed and unacknowledged, and they show their heads at the most unexpected and sometimes inopportune times. In this chapter, we look first at different ways we journey—tourist, traveler, invader, and resident—before surveying different kinds of journeys—adventures, missions, odysseys, and various types of wanderings, even when they take us through the darkest valleys.

I have come to believe that the kind of journey we are on and the way we journey have profound spiritual implications for the way we understand and deal with the tensions between going home and staying away, looking back and leaning forward, and developing roots and wings. The prophets have much to teach us in this regard. Isaiah instructs us to *walk* in the light of the Lord (2:5), and to *walk* in the way, whether we turn to the right or the left (30:21). Jeremiah counsels that when we *walk* in the good way, we find rest (6:16), and Micah adds that we are to *walk* humbly with God. In the New Testament, we find this affirmation from John, "But if we *walk* in the light, as he is in the light, we have fellowship with one another . . ." (1 John 1:7). There is much counsel for us to draw from these wise voices, but at the very least it is this: we are to *walk*. Don't just stand there—*walk*!

## Tourists, Travelers, Invaders, and Residents

I remember a particular faculty lunch from 1990 as if it were yesterday. Four of us were sitting together, laughing, teasing, and regaling whoever would listen with stories from our pasts. Some of the stories were probably true; some of them were certainly exaggerations. Somehow, we fell upon the subject of travel in strange lands, and we discovered that we, all four of us, had been to Viet Nam at one time or another, but the descriptions of our experiences there were remarkably different.

One of us was on a cruise from Hong Kong to Singapore, and the ship made four stops in Viet Nam. At each stop, the tourists disembarked, climbed into tour buses, and visited local museums, sites of interest, and reminders of the war with the US. By mid-afternoon, the buses returned to the ship, allowing plenty of time for a swim in the pool before dressing up for an onboard dinner buffet with the captain.

Another of us did some traveling across Viet Nam, conducting research on the post-war experiences and challenges faced by those who had sided with the Americans during the war, and were left to make their own way when the Americans pulled out. The research project turned out to be a difficult and painful task, involving several months of home stays with families. As trust and friendships developed, families began to share their stories of discrimination, exclusion, re-education, torture, and even the death of family members and close friends. This was a much deeper engagement—the journey of a traveler, not a tourist.

A third colleague at the table just smiled a sad smile and told us that his job in Viet Nam was to make swimming pools for the US Navy. He went on to explain that he was a bomber pilot, and he flew one or two missions each day. When their efforts were evaluated later that day, the bomb craters looked like big swimming pools. Then, he went to dinner and had a stiff drink—or two. He shared that he still had nightmares about those swimming pools. He wasn't a tourist or traveler in Viet Nam. Instead, he was part of a process to impose the will of the US forces, intending to offer a new way of life to the people. Invaders make few lasting relationships with the people that they are trying to change. They come, they occupy, and at some point or another, they leave.

The last colleague noted that his experience in Viet Nam was totally different from all the rest. He was a Quaker and a conscientious objector, and first went to Viet Nam during the height of the conflict to stand with the locals as best he could. He volunteered in a small village in the south, teaching school and working in an orphanage for displaced children. After the war, he returned to Viet Nam as soon as he could and started a school, teaching reading, writing, and job skills to children of all ages. He stayed there for over a decade, returning to this country because of a serious illness. He taught intercultural studies at the university with a passion, not as a tourist, traveler, or invader, but as a resident who knew and loved the children who knew and loved him, too. He said that he could not wait to return to his adopted "home." In fact, he did, and he is buried there. He became a permanent resident.

It seems to me that as we journey through life, we have choices to make. We can be a tourist, seeing the sights and eating a meal here and there, but remaining totally insulated from those cultures around us. Usually, there are some things we learn but we are not changed deeply as a result of such experiences. Or we can be travelers, taking time to develop trust and friendships with others, becoming part of their families. This, it seems to me, is a more helpful and satisfying way to journey. Of course, we can also be invaders, just dropping in and releasing a bomb or two, hoping to influence the local culture and make it more like what we are used to or what we enjoy. Or we can become residents with our neighbors, fully engaged in their culture, living with them—not holding them at arm's length or trying to remake them in our own image. We get to choose how we journey.

I want to focus in just a bit more on the ways we travel spiritually, especially when it comes to attending church. We can be tourists, just checking in from time to time and catching the highlights without any engagement whatsoever. Many times, it is simply a "one and done" experience, in for some coffee, a song or two, then out the door. We can be travelers, staying a bit longer and making a few friends, but without any intention of staying around for the long haul or contributing in any meaningful way. Some describe this approach as dating. And, sadly, some of us choose to be invaders. Not interested in engaging or honoring the local culture, we simply arrive, fully intent on remaking the church to reflect our own theology and manner of worship (or to add a hymn or get rid of the drums). It's a bumpy way to travel. But we can also choose to become residents, joining in with the intent of staying put, serving, and proclaiming that these are my people—for better or worse. And over time, you will likely experience both, but you stay anyway because this church has become your home. You know the people there, and they know you.

Tourists, travelers, invaders, or residents. We get to choose how we attend church, too.

## Different Ways to Journey

Throughout this chapter, we have been considering the idea of journey, and I have suggested that we are all on one—of one kind or another. Not only are there different types of travelers (tourist, traveler, invader, or resident), there are also different types of travels (adventures, missions, odysseys, and wanderings). While I clearly acknowledge that some types of travelers are more engaged and engaging than others, particularly when it comes to finding and maintaining a church home, the same may not be true when it comes to types of travels. As we will see, they all have distinct rewards, and each can have a shadow side, too. Thus, there are profound spiritual implications for the type of journey we are on. One is not necessarily better than the other, and at different times during our adult years, many of us embark on different types of spiritual travels.

To be honest, I do not try to connect all the dots when I discuss the spiritual implications of most of the meditations in this book, leaving the personal applications for you, the reader, to make. I do, however, chime in with my opinion in what follows because I earnestly believe that how we journey does matter, and it is easy to end up in a ditch of one kind or another if we lose our way. Thankfully, there is a gentle guide who is with us, even through our darkest valleys and in our deepest ditches.

## *Adventures*

A safari, a theme park, a wilderness hike, a risky climb, a big concert, a bungee jump, a trip to an unfamiliar, even dangerous, place—these are all forms of adventures. They are thrilling. They make you feel alive. They get your heart rate up. They are out of the ordinary, and they are fun.

Some travelers spend a lifetime chasing the next exciting thing, the next high, always on the go. It can be an exhilarating way to live, from one mountain peak to the next, always after whatever is next—anything to fight the boredom that can accompany much of daily life. The shadow side, however, is that chasing the next "wow" can be uprooting, tiring, and hard on relationships of all kinds. When your focus is on "what I want to experience," those close to you can easily become ways and means for your own adventures, and the imbalance—high on experience and low on relationships—can take a toll. And sadly, even chasing the next high can become boring after a while.

I must admit that I worry some about spiritual adventurists, too. The positive side is that those after and attuned to a spiritual adventure are more likely to step out in faith, leaning into opportunities and possibilities that most of us would count as reckless, even dangerous. And in doing so, good things are sometimes accomplished. But a spiritual adventure can quickly become a wild-goose chase, without direction, expending a great deal of time, energy, and resources, chasing after the latest program or ministry opportunity.

It seems to me that many in leadership are particularly attracted to spiritual adventures of one kind or another for one reason or another, when in fact what those who follow honestly and earnestly need are direction from a gentle guide and care from a good shepherd. If we are not intentional about the work before us, the adventure of the bright lights of worship on Sunday mornings can take priority in time, attention, and resources over the behind-the-scenes work that goes on during the week in small groups, through service opportunities, and in one-to-one care, mentoring, and spiritual direction, even though it is there that the hard work of spiritual formation, comfort, and encouragement takes place.

Surely, the life of faith is an adventure of sorts, and we ought to lean into opportunities to see God at work in us and through us in new and incredible ways. However, I doubt that a three-ring circus, characterized by a bewildering variety of events or activities, is a productive way to shape and form that life of faith, regardless of the thrill and attention that comes to the ringmaster.

## *Missions and Odysseys*

Missions and odysseys are related journeys. Both can be described as a long trip or period involving several different activities and challenges. The difference, it seems to me, is that when we are on a mission, there is a specific outcome in mind, whereas an odyssey is a journey in search of something, even though it may not be known what that something is. In an odyssey, the old saying, "I'll know it when I see it," is more than just an old saying. We can be drawn to this type of journey, knowing or hoping that we will find what we are looking for or what we are looking for will find us, before we make our way back home.

Being on a mission provides direction, focus, and persistence, and the missionally possessed among us keep our attention on what is important, particularly on what is important to them. There are those who have a persistent passion for the homeless, childcare, the poor, or those marginalized in one way or another around the globe, or for safe drinking water, compassionate immigration, healthcare reform, or the minimum wage. The list can go on and on. Whatever it is, it is their mission and they won't let go—nor should they. They keep all of us reminded of real needs that can easily go unnoticed and unaddressed. Every church needs believers on a mission.

However, a mission can easily turn into a crusade, an activity that is so singularly intent on a desired outcome that those who stand in the way don't stand a chance. In essence, those on a crusade become single-issue advocates, even though the local congregation may have many needs before them, and not all their attention and resources can be focused on just one issue. Sometimes, those on a mission can be frustrating to those in leadership, and those in leadership can be frustrating to the mission folk. This can be a healthy tension, but it has to be acknowledged and negotiated or discontent and disillusionment will fester.

An odyssey is like a mission in many ways, but it is far less focused, usually not about addressing a single issue. Rather, it is a journey or even a series of journeys in search of something or compelled by something, something in need of restoration or recovery. More often than not, those on an odyssey feel a distinct draw to the journey without being fully able to explain what exactly is compelling them to go, but it is real.

Another distinction between mission and odyssey is that those on a mission are never satisfied, never complete. There's always more to do. It is always before them; the mission is never over. Those on an odyssey, however, do have an end in sight—home. Wherever the odyssey takes them, home is always on the mind, even though as we will discuss a bit later in this chapter, many times those on an odyssey find returning home to be difficult process. Things have changed. Either home has changed, or they have—or both. Home, as we shall see, is not an easy destination.

Many of us are on a spiritual odyssey, leaving home, the safety of our religious heritage, for something out there that beckons us to come. It is an uncertain and uneasy journey at times, since we are not able to put into words what we are after, but we know that we are lacking something that brings peace and gives meaning to our lives—something beyond a good job and a busy weekend. We bounce from church to church, or stop attending altogether, but we feel a spiritual tug to keep looking. Some of us find a church, or a church finds us, that provides what we have been looking and hoping for, and when we do we are thankful. For others, however, the odyssey is much longer, sometimes an entire lifetime. I don't have any profound advice for such an odyssey other than to keep making your way, keep looking, and keep heading for home. Jesus told the story of the prodigal son. This son went on quite an odyssey, too, but after assessing his dismal situation, "he got up and went to his father. But while he was a long way off, his father saw him and was filled with compassion for him; he ran to his son, threw his arm around him and kissed him" (Luke 15:20).

I particularly like two aspects of this story. First, the son didn't have to make it all the way home. While *he was still a long way off*, the father came running in a full sprint, one sandal flying off and his robe flapping in the wind! That's good news for all of us who are on a spiritual odyssey of one kind or another. When we turn toward home, the father will come running to us. And the second aspect is this: the father didn't make the son go behind the house and take a bath or visit the local synagogue or go through some type of purification ritual to be ceremonially clean before he was properly presented and received. Instead, the father gave him a huge hug, kissed him, and threw a party. The son was greeted—warts and baggage and stink and all—just as he was, and it wasn't a pretty picture. The good news for all of us who odyssey is that the father will take us just as we are, too, warts and baggage and stink and all. All we have to do is turn toward home and the Father will take care of the celebration.

## *Wanderings*

There are all kinds of names for those who wander—nomads, itinerants, rovers, even marauders, to name just a few. The common denominator, of course, is that wonderers are not trying to make their way back home. Rather, the journey *is* their home. Home travels with them. These journeys are often characterized as irresponsible, immature, and reckless. Perhaps some wanderings are just that, but I think wandering gets a bad name. I believe that wandering can be a deeply formative spiritual practice, a response to a divine summons to move on, to let go, to be confident that new things can be discovered without fear of getting lost. Wanderers are not fearful of losing sight of home since home is in the journey. However, wandering does require a sense of true north, a spiritual sensitivity to what is ultimately important, for it is certainly possible to lose your way even when there is no set destination. Truly, all who wander are not lost, but honestly, some are.

Thus far, we have discussed spiritual adventures, missions, and odysseys, and I have suggested that there are spiritual implications for each kind of journey, both positive and negative. But what about wandering? Are there spiritual implications for wanderings, too? I believe the answer is yes. For starters, those who wander are more attuned to the road and to those who do not fit easily or comfortably into more permanent social settings. They are more likely to notice and care for the disenfranchised, since they have experienced the alienation and disaffection that accompanies wandering. They see things that others do not, and people that others do not. And wanderers have seen and are open to many different ways of interpreting life with God. These insights, I have come to believe, are valuable gifts to any Christian faith community. They expand our insights and stretch our imaginations and interpretations of what God can do and what God calls us to do. This is, indeed, good.

However, wandering can generate its own biases and preconceptions, too, particularly against religious structures and authorities, seeing formal religious activities and congregations as excessive, even unnecessary. All who wander are not lost, to be sure, but neither are all who establish permanent residence in a faith community. It is easy to marginalize those who do not walk your path.

In this section, we have considered different types of travelers and different types of spiritual journeys, thinking together about what it truly means to walk with God. We noted that each type of journey has its particular strengths, and a shadow side, too. I am convinced that it would be helpful to all of us if we appreciated our own local faith community as a collection of travelers, giving everyone the space to chart their own path as best they can, and to remember that we really do need each other. In one way or another, we are all trying to get home before dark.

## Dark Valleys

Before we end our discussion of metaphors that describe our spiritual journeys, several questions beg to be addressed: what about the detours and diversions we face when we journey, and how are we to face the darkest of times—even the Valley of Death? Surely, we, all of us, will experience a detour or roadblock along the way, and maybe more than one.

Yes, if we journey, detours and roadblocks will appear—you can count on it. Life is messy: either it is, has been, or will be. I honestly wish that it were not so, but it is. Regardless of how carefully and closely we follow God's leading, the road we travel at some point or another will be bumpy. So, what can we say about the detours that come our way? First, a detour does not mean that you have lost your way or that you have done something wrong. God is not mad at you. Detours do come, to be sure, but they are not a form of divine retribution. There is more than enough bad luck, unkindness, selfishness, stupidity, self-seeking, and evil in this world to account for the detours we face. God doesn't work that way. When we consider our detours and disappointments as punishment from an angry and vengeful God, we diminish God's love and grace for us, and we minimize the part we play in our own journeys, too. Remember—life is messy.

Second, roadblocks and detours come in all shapes and sizes. Some are small and benign, mostly irritating, really. They take us on a different road, but our spirits are intact and our journey continues. Others, however, represent a major disruption for our journey, things like a serious illness, a public failure, an intimate rejection, or a serious loss—in our relationships, our hopes, our dreams, our courage, our perspective, our voice, or even our sense of direction. Such disruptions often lead to discouragement and disorientation, and we can easily lose our way, deciding that the journey is over or not worth the effort. When we face such detours, even our darkest and most dreaded valleys, it is crucial to be mindful that while life is messy, God is faithful. When the detours of life take us through the darkest of valleys—even the Valley of Death—God is with us, bringing hope and healing and courage to the most painful and disruptive experiences we face. We are never left to journey on our own.

And since we know that detours are bound to arise, it is important to journey with a support system in place—caring friends, honest mentors, and a supportive faith community, even when we wander. When God looked at Adam and said, "It is not good for man to be alone" (Gen 2:18), I honestly believe that it was the journey of life that God had in mind. As we journey, we are mindful that detours will come, that we need a caring support system, and that God is with us always, even in our darkest valleys.

## Scripture

Before we end this chapter with some words of practical advice and some questions for reflection and discussion, let's look at three journeys described in Scripture—two from the Old Testament (Abraham and Jacob) and one from the New Testament (Jesus). As we will see, they were all on a spiritual journey of one kind or another.

## Abraham—Odyssey

"By faith, Abraham, when called to go to a place that he would later receive as his inheritance, obeyed and went, even though he did not know where he was going. By faith he made his home in the promised land like a stranger in a foreign country . . ." (Heb 11:8–9). If there was ever an apt example of an odyssey, this is it. Remember, an odyssey is a long trip, full of different challenges and obstacles to overcome, and having a destination that is not entirely clear. In many instances, you won't know the destination until you get there, just as Abraham obeyed and went, *even though he did not know where he was going.* In many respects, the promised land found Abraham, not the other way around.

And when Abraham reached the promised land, he lived in a tent like a nomad, like a foreigner in a strange land. As it turns out, even getting to "home," wherever that is and whatever that means, is not necessarily an easy place to be. Odysseys change people, and home rarely lives up to the memories we carry. There's a spiritual lesson here for all of us who feel compelled to journey. The odyssey will change you, too, and even if you can find it, home may be a difficult place to reside. Often, those on a spiritual odyssey end up on a second journey in search of a new home. Please hear me—this is not a bad thing—but it is a real thing, a reality to be acknowledged and addressed with love and care and grace, especially with those who have looked forward to your return for some time. Things are often different; your piece just doesn't fit the puzzle anymore. Still, it is good to make peace with that place called home, even if you can no longer reside there.

## Jacob—Wandering

Genesis, the first book in the Old Testament, tells the story of Jacob and Esau. When Jacob left home at the urging of his mother, it was not to undertake a spiritual odyssey or to respond to a summons from God. No, he fled, running away from his brother in fear of his life, and his fears were well-earned. Since he cheated his older brother twice, home was no longer a safe place, so he took off with what he could carry and made his way to some distant relatives far away. There he worked to establish a home and a future, but you have to wonder if he didn't always keep one eye on the horizon for any sign of his brother heading his way. Bad decisions have a trajectory of their own; they take you somewhere, and the memories don't easily go away.

His life had its share of ups and downs. If he were to describe himself today, he would say, "I am not a perfect man," which was painfully obvious. Still, despite the bumps and bruises, he did well on the farm and kept thinking about home. Finally, regardless of the outcome, he decided to head for home for good. Even in this he was a bit cowardly, sending the women and children ahead to meet his brother first, hoping to generate some sympathy and goodwill. In the end, it was unnecessary. Esau was overjoyed to have his brother back, and the homecoming was good. The prodigal brother had returned.

The good news here is that sometimes it is possible to go home, even if we leave home on a dead run. Surely, the journey, however it starts, will change us, but sometimes what we encounter and how we grow makes us even more appreciative of what home has to offer. This is good news, indeed.

## Jesus—Mission

If there is any agreement among the four Gospels about anything, it is this: Jesus was on a mission. I think it is fair to say that he struggled with this mission from time to time, even praying for a different outcome if at all possible (Matt 26:39; Mark 14:36; Luke 4:34), but he was committed to the mission. "My food" said Jesus, "is to do the will of him who sent me and to finish his work" (John 4:34). He meant it, and he did.

Those of us who feel a calling or carry a burden know that being on a spiritual mission can be daunting, and at times discouraging. Most of us have been tempted to take a "time out" from the grind of the duties and responsibilities from time to time, but more often than not, even when we are ready to let the mission go, the mission will not let us go. When we're on a mission, the word of the day is to keep walking, even when the outcome is unknown or the peril is known with certainty.

### Some Practical Advice

Let me end this chapter on journey with three words of practical advice. I readily concede that they are not earthshaking, but hopefully they will be helpful to those of us who journey or those who long for one.

First, before we can go, we have to be willing to let go, to lose sight of the shore and all that is safe for a very long time. This can be unnerving, but it is necessary.

Second, be aware that journeys will shape any of us who venture out. While it is good to have an end in mind when we journey, at the end of the day, it is what happens on the journey that matters far more than reaching the destination. It is on the journey that we are shaped and formed in the image of Christ.

Finally, regardless of the journey and where we're at on the journey, how we treat others along the way always matters. I have come to believe that kindness is the virtue that drives and undergirds all the others. Kindness invites hospitality, compassion, and humility, the things we need to carry and exercise if we want to be shaped along the way as we make our way toward home.

## Conclusion

We started this chapter by observing that most of us are on a journey, a spiritual journey, of one kind or another, and if the prophets have anything to tell us, it is this: don't just stand there, walk! That's good advice. We examined different types of journeyers (tourist, traveler, invader, and resident) and different kinds of journeys (adventures, missions, odysseys, and wanderings). We noted that each way to journey has positive aspects and a shadow side. It is important to be aware of the way we travel and the why of our travels, too, because they will shape us.

We discussed the reality that detours will find us, even terrible ones, but God is faithful, even in our darkest valleys. We then considered the journeys of Abraham (odyssey), Jacob (wandering), and Jesus (mission), noting that finding home is possible, but not always easy or comfortable. Then, three words of practical advice were offered: (1) If you're going to set out on a journey, you have to be willing to lose sight of the shore; (2) journeys are formative—it is on the journey that we are shaped and formed in the image of Christ; and (3) how we treat others on the journey is more important than the journey itself. Kindness is king.

I want to share two final thoughts as we conclude this meditation on journey. As John Steinbeck noted, people don't take trips—trips take people. We have far less control of our journeys than we would like to admit, but there it is. Journeys require trust. And finally, it is important to remember that we are not on a journey to find God. Rather, we are on a journey with God, and that makes all the difference. Travel well.

## Questions for Reflection and Discussion:

1. When it comes to church attendance, are you a tourist, traveler, invader, or resident? How so?

2. Are you on a spiritual journey? If so, would you describe it as an adventure, an odyssey, a mission, or just wandering? Explain.

3. This chapter began with the assertion that we all feel a tension between the desire to be at home and the desire to journey. What has the greatest pull on you—roots or wings? Why do you think that this is so?

4. Do you agree that how we treat others on the journey is more important than the journey itself? Why or why not?

5. Is trust an issue for you, especially trust in God? Why or why not?

## Psalm 23

The LORD is my shepherd; I shall not want.

He makes me lie down in green pastures; He leads me beside still waters.

He restores my soul; He leads me in paths of righteousness for His name's sake.

Even though I walk through the valley of the shadow of death . . .

# CHAPTER 8

## *I Will Fear No Evil—Courage*

Life is mostly froth and bubble, two things stand like stone.
Kindness in another's trouble, courage in your own.
—ADAM LINDSAY GORDON

### Introduction

This may be the most uncomfortable meditation in this book to read, let alone embrace. It was certainly the most difficult chapter for me to write. I struggled with what themes to include and what to ignore, and what to say about the ones I chose. I did not, and do not, wish to sound silly, simplistic, or moralistic, but I do believe that the metaphors and approaches we use to understand and cope with the evil we see in the world and in our own lives deserves an honest assessment, especially so if we wish to be led by the gentle guide and the good shepherd. Please note that as we have already observed, the gentle guide and good shepherd are metaphors that help us understand God's work in our lives. And as I will suggest, we use metaphors to portray evil, too, and they can either clarify or confuse our thinking about holy living.

Still, it is not easy to write about evil, even though it is a reality that we all have experienced or carry with us. It was even difficult to come up with a tentative outline, something that usually flows for me. Why so? I believe that one reason the topic of evil is so difficult to discuss is that it is so intensely personal, and in our culture, we hold such things closely, out of public view, and oddly enough, especially in church. We put on a smiley face, sing with gusto, pass the peace, and then go out to lunch. No place for confessions of evil in such a setting.

On one level, I get that. There's no reason to share such things unless it is a safe place to do so, and corporate worship may not be that safe of a space—too public. On another level, however, if we cannot have a serious conversation about the fact that we have all sinned and fallen short of God's glory, that we are all sinners saved by grace, in the context of our own faith community, where on earth are these confessions to be offered and honestly addressed? Sadly, for many of us, the answer is "nowhere," so we simply ignore it, hoping that it will not see the light of day. This reality makes a chapter such as this uncomfortable, but in my view, necessary. To begin, we start with some general observations about fear before examining several ways that many of us deal with the evil we face in our daily lives, and how we can practice courage as we journey toward wholeness and home. First, however, let me share four encounters from my own experience when I was confronted by or confronted individuals with the deep fear of evil, the very thing that the writer of the Twenty-third Psalm affirms as unnecessary—*I will fear no evil*!

## Christian University Encounters

I had the privilege of serving as an administrator at several fine Christian universities. I can testify that they are filled and supported by good people, earnest people. The vignettes that follow are drawn from experiences at four of them. I have attempted to recount these encounters as faithfully and factually as possible without betraying anyone's identity. As we will see, fear comes in many forms, and forms us in many ways. Some are healthy; some not so much.

### *Telling the Truth*

A freshman student knocked on my office door and started talking before I could even open the door. "My roommate is a thief!" he blurted out, and then told me that his bank called to warn him that someone was using his checking account and forging his signature. It turned out to be his roommate, who stole a few of his personal checks, made the checks out to himself, forged his roommate's signature, and cashed the checks at the university's business office—using his school ID. Thus, there was no doubt that he was the culprit.

When I confronted the roommate about the check forgeries, he first denied any involvement and argued that his signature on the back of the check didn't *exactly* match his own. However, when I explained that he had used his own school ID and the cashier affirmed that he was the one who cashed the checks, he looked at me and said: "OK, I did it. It would be unchristian to lie about it. I don't want the evil one to ever get the best of me." For one of the few times in my life, I was absolutely speechless. As I look back, I guess I could have said, "Too late on that concern," but I didn't. He left school that day and didn't return. I've often wondered how his theology held up in the long run.

### Soul Snatchers

Two concerned parents angrily pushed their way into my office during freshman orientation, with a demand that I immediately go over to the bookstore and remove a poster from the front window. It seems that there was a poster advertising a retrospective of the 1960s by a prominent Christian author, and the book cover displayed a series of photos, one of which was a band of anti-war protestors holding signs. One included the circular peace sign. The peace sign was no more than a square inch, but this couple wanted the poster immediately removed before any other students happened to see it.

Innocently, I tried to understand their concern. I asked if it had something to do with the notion that to protest the war was unpatriotic and unchristian. They assured me that this wasn't their immediate concern, so I asked if it had something to do with the alternative lifestyles often advocated as part of the 60s. Again, the answer was no, although they did have some sympathies for an indictment of this way of living. Finally, I looked the parents right in the eyes and asked, "What, then, is your concern? I don't get it." They shook their heads in disbelief and said, "It's that New Age peace sign. We're afraid that our son will walk by, see that sign, and lose his soul to the devil." I was silent for some time as we all stared at the sidewalk. I finally asked for clarification: "Are you saying that you are afraid that your son, who is a faithful Christian, will merely look at that tiny peace sign as he walks by the bookstore and the devil will somehow reach out and snatch his soul? That your son's faith in the

God of the universe is so weak that it can be stolen away with a glance at a book poster?" "The devil only needs the slightest opening," was their response. "We need to protect our son from seeing anything that might threaten his spiritual journey. The world is a dangerous place." I smiled a sad smile and said, "I don't think you can go through life acting like blinders for your son, and I don't think that's very helpful even if you could."

Later that day, they withdrew their son from school and returned home. I've often wondered what became of him and his faith, a faith that needed to be constantly protected from everything, and I wonder how his parents managed their own lives in such a way.

### *I Only Want to Learn What I Already Believe*

A freshman stood just outside my door, pacing back and forth. As soon as I got off the phone, my administrative assistant came in and asked if I had just a few minutes to talk to a very frustrated student. I did, of course, and I welcomed her and offered a seat at the round table by the bay window in my office. After giving her name, she began to cry and said that she was uncertain if she could remain in school. It wasn't the usual culprits—financial aid, a roommate conflict, or illness. No, this had to do with her Introduction to the Bible course, Bible 100. She was deeply disturbed that it was suggested that Moses may not have been the author of the entire Pentateuch, the first five book of the Old Testament, that David might not have written all the psalms attributed to him, and that the Gospels were most likely not authored in order—Matthew, Mark, Luke, and John. She shook her head and said, "I only want to be taught what I already believe, because if what I believe is not entirely true, then my faith is worthless—all of it, and I'll end up in spiritual ruins in the clutches of the devil."

My first thought was to point out that attending a university of any kind, especially a fine Christian university, would be rather pointless if the only objective was to confirm what you already knew and believed, but I kept that response to myself. Instead, I told her that learning in a healthy environment like a Christian university with mature, wise, Christian faculty and staff was precisely the place to be challenged, to adjust and grow in wisdom, knowledge, *and* faith. They were not at odds or mutually exclusive. We needn't be afraid to explore new ideas or adjust what we believe. Faith and learning, I explained, were two sides of the same coin.

Honestly, I don't know if my statements made any sense to her or if they had any impact whatsoever. I do know that she stayed in school for the remainder of the semester and stopped by my office to say goodbye in December. She told me that she was transferring to a "safe" college, far away from any form of evil, where faith *is* the issue, not learning. I wished her well, and I didn't hear from her again. I've often wondered what became of her and her faith, too.

## *Glimpses and Addictions*

I had a suspicion that I was in for a difficult conversation when the father of a current student, a junior, was sitting in the office waiting room with an Art History text book on his lap and a dozen or so sticky notes on display throughout the text. As I surmised, he was upset by some of the "pornography" that his son had been exposed to in the text. Upon further discussions, he made it clear that any view of the human body below the neck, real or in pictures, was inappropriate and evil, and it had to be eradicated. That is to say, this particular art text and some of the professor's slides needed to be immediately banned—and then destroyed before the devil destroyed more young souls. This led to at least six extended conversations, but the issue remained the same. I was even named a sinner since I wouldn't ban the book, and my resignation was demanded by the father and his pastor. This, along with some very nasty anonymous letters sent to my boss, members of the Board of Trustees, and local clergy, made a resolution very difficult—and very public.

As I pressed for the reason for all the fear and rage, the father told me that his older son was addicted to pornography and drugs, and he was sure that it all started innocently with ads on TV. He was now in prison, so the father was doing everything he could do to protect his younger son from the evil one who intended to ruin his entire family. Honestly, I hurt for this father, but tried as best I could to convince him that seeing a picture of Michael Angelo's David in an Art History text book and viewing pornography were two very different things, and that he was confusing any view of the human body, real or a statue or a painting, with evil. The beauty of art was an inspiration, a blessing, not a curse or a trap set by the evil one.

As you might suspect, my argument did not prove to be persuasive, and he told me that if I didn't comply with his demands, he would have no alternative but to remove his son from school and keep him at home—literally. I pleaded with the father to consider his son's experience at the university. I said that his son was a second semester junior and would soon be graduating, and from all I could tell, he was doing well and loving every minute of it, even serving on several ministry teams and leading a Bible study with his apartment mates. The kingdom needed him, and his soul could not just be snatched away. We Christians were not meant to live in constant fear.

His father finally relented (with a great deal of reluctance) but made it clear that the responsibility for his son's soul now rested squarely on my shoulders. I accepted the responsibility, knowing full well that God is faithful, and an Art 100 course would not lead to his son's damnation. Fourteen months later, I had the privilege of signing his diploma and congratulating him as he walked across the stage at commencement. He is now in ministry and I trust that his father is a bit less fearful and a bit more trusting. He was trying so hard to save his family from the evil one, but his fears blinded him. He could not see the beauty in the human figure or in art of any kind, for that matter, even classic pieces dedicated to expressing the glory of God.

\* \* \*

What these four stories have in common, of course, is fear—fear of evil, and it isn't a healthy kind of fear. Going through life fearing that your soul can be snatched away for the slightest reason or no reason at all is not abundant living in any way, shape, or form. It is tyranny, and it is unnecessary. In what follows, we'll talk about dealing with the fear of evil and how courage can be fruitfully practiced.

## Fearing Evil

"I will fear no evil." What a bold, even audacious, statement. With all that is going on in our world, how can we not fear evil, that which is all around us and in us, too? For starters, this affirmation from Psalm 23 does not say that we should never be afraid or that fear is necessarily a bad thing. It is not. There are many times when we should be afraid—when considering riding out an approaching hurricane or standing directly in front of an approaching mob or a speeding truck. Fear keeps us out of all kinds of troubles and difficulties. Without the fear of being caught and having to come home and face my parents, who knows where I might have gone and what I might have done during my high school years. Fear can be a healthy restraint from pursuing unwise and detrimental paths.

But fear of evil is another thing altogether. Why? The simple answer is that it just doesn't help, at least not in the way we would like. Evil is real. We know that, but it is hard to pin down, hard to describe, hard to talk about, and even harder to admit that it is at work within us—and in our institutions, too, even our churches. The specter of evil can raise its ugly head almost anywhere, and it does, so it must be confronted—but not feared. That's where courage comes in.

A bit more complicated answer to this question is that we use metaphors to try to describe and explain the unexplainable, things like the nature of God and the existence of evil, to name two biggies. That's why the Twenty-third Psalm is so full of metaphors—shepherd, guide, host, green pastures, still waters, paths of righteousness, the valley of death, a table set before our enemies, an overflowing cup, and a head anointed with oil, to name just a few. It is the psalmist's way of trying to express in words a deeply personal experience with God. Metaphors substitute for that which cannot be explained fully literally, and as such, they are helpful but always imperfect, incomplete, and sometimes misleading. The metaphors we carry about God and about evil are profoundly personal, and they shape us in ways known and unknown.

Two popular metaphors for evil come quickly to mind: a personal metaphor (the devil or evil one) and an overarching metaphor (spiritual warfare). I must admit that I get nervous about these metaphors. Honestly, I don't think that they are helpful. Let me explain. To personify evil, calling it the work of the devil, can offer some explanation about how evil works, but it can also remove us from responsibility for addressing it. To put it bluntly, to say that "the devil made me do it" or "the devil may snatch her soul" is to give evil far more credit and power than it is due, and it removes a clear sense of personal responsibility for our own decisions and actions. I think the story of Job has much to do with this distortion. I don't believe for a minute that God entered into conversations with the evil one out of idle curiosity, and then let all hell break loose on Job and his family as a way of testing his faith, some sort of a cosmic contest. Of course, the writer of Job is trying to understand and express why bad things happen to good people, a subject that has been discussed for thousands of years, but personifying evil in this way can lead to fear and a sense of helplessness. Remember, we join the psalmist in affirming, "I will fear *no* evil."

The metaphor of spiritual warfare has similar consequences. Of course, things happen—bad things—and we, all of us, are trying to understand what is happening to us, around us, and in us. It is an immensely complex undertaking, so the notion that a war is going on in the spiritual realm does offer some insight. Certainly, anyone who is honest will admit that they battle with evil from time to time, but that doesn't mean that there is a spiritual reality where battles rage as in the time of King David. I am concerned that such an understanding of evil—at war with God (and we are the bystanders, and sometimes hit by salvoes from the enemy and sometimes by friendly fire)—leaves us alone, uncertain, caught in the middle, spiritually dependent, and afraid, just the opposite of living abundantly. Such an understanding of warfare with evil can draw individuals, even groups, into an intense focus on such things as needing divine protection, exorcisms, fighting the devil, and spiritual bodyguards and superheroes. When this happens the world becomes a very fearful place, a spiritual war zone, even on the way to the grocery store. Such a metaphor for evil leaves all of us in a very dangerous world, in need of "powerful spiritual defenders" in order to safely make our way home. That is counter to all I know about God as the good shepherd and the gentle guide.

## Dealing with Evil

So, if it is not helpful to personify evil or conceive of it as the central element in a cosmic spiritual battle, then how do we deal with the evil that is around us, and at times, within us.? For starters, we don't deny that evil exists. It does. We can't excuse our behavior by saying, "I wasn't myself today" or "that wasn't really me." In fact, that was you. We start by telling the truth about the shortcomings in our own Christian walk rather than stowing them away in the attic along with our luggage and an old set of golf clubs. They are out of sight, but they don't go away. Sooner or later, they will fester and see the light of day. We start by being courageous enough to be honest. We do deal with evil. All of us.

And neither do we try to excuse evil. It is so easy to justify little transgressions—it was just a little white lie, it didn't really hurt anyone that much, they'll get their turn the next time, everyone cheats a little bit, I've done so much that I deserve it, they won't miss it . . . Sadly, we speak of the deceiver when actually we act selfishly and only deceive ourselves. We confront evil when we look directly in the mirror, face the reality of our own thoughts and actions, and make amends when necessary.

At the end of the day, we can't wish evil away. We can't ignore it, we can't deny it, and we shouldn't accommodate it—it must be squarely faced. When we decide to follow Christ and join others who claim Christ, it is the beginning of a long journey to holy living. Along the way, a fair share of quick fixes will be offered: a right belief, the right baptism, a right practice, the right day to worship, the right way to worship, the right way to take communion, the right diet, the right language, a trip to the altar (or two), and so on. Please hear me, I am not trying to trivialize such matters. They do shape us in many ways and provide what sociologists call social cohesion, bonds that link members of a social group to one another and to the group as a whole. But I do say this: beware of the quick fix or any special requirements for membership or entree into the inner circle that demand a specific belief or loyalty or action. Such an approach to Christian fellowship quickly creates a world of "us vs. them," and fear of others or the outside (evil) is the glue that holds everything together.

Jesus sent out his disciples with this caution, "I am sending you out like sheep among wolves. Therefore be as shrewd as snakes and as innocent as doves" (Matt 10:16). Sheep among wolves—that sounds to me like they will have to deal with evil, and the instructions are to be a *shrewd* and *innocent*. The word *shrewd* means to be astute, smart, intelligent, perceptive, and wise. And to be innocent means to be guiltless, blameless, unimpeachable, and above suspicion. This says to me that as we go about our days evil will be present, and we are instructed to have a clean heart and a clear head, to be holy and wise, regardless of what metaphors we use to describe what we encounter. Providentially, we are not left on our own. We have a gentle guide to walk with us as we make our way home, but if we are to fear no evil, one more thing must be summoned—courage.

## Courage

I think some of us have more inclination to lean into difficult situations than the rest of us. That is to say, great courage is not something that most of us are necessarily born with, but as Maya Angelou suggests, we do have the potential, the seed, the spark, to become courageous—or at least to be more so. Courage is both a virtue and a spiritual practice, and as with any virtue or practice, it grows with intentional use and shapes us in good ways as it does. In short, the spiritual practice of courage invites more courage.

We begin with the assertion that we will fear no evil, and we exercise that confidence when we summon the courage to face evil right where we live, right in our own backyards. Rather than entering into some type of grand cosmic battle against the forces of evil, I think the place to start is to be discerning as we go about our days, to be holy *and* wise when we see ideologies, theologies, practices, and actions that divide, polarize, and marginalize our neighbors, and our churches. Simply put, the spiritual practice of courage begins when we assert that we fear no evil and ask God daily for discernment to recognize the injustice, exclusion, and intolerance that we encounter in our day-to-day activities, and then summon the courage to speak against them—to lean in with courage. As we summon courage, we find that evil is not to be feared but to be named for what it is. This spiritual practice draws on a reservoir of strength that shapes and forms us as it is bidden. And we never do this alone—we have a gentle guide who leads us. We can trust the journey.

## Scripture

I want each of us to read this passage, this courageous proclamation from the Apostle Paul in his letter to the churches in Rome, three times—slowly, and let the questions sink in: "Who shall separate us from the love of Christ? Shall trouble or hardship or persecution or famine or nakedness or danger or sword? . . . No, in all these things we are more than conquerors through him who loved us. For I am convinced that neither death nor life, neither angels nor demons, neither the present nor the future, nor any powers, neither height nor depth, nor anything else in all creation, will be able to separate us from the love of God that is in Christ Jesus our Lord" (Rom 8:35–39).

Who and what can separate us from the love of God—trouble, hardship, persecution, famine, nakedness, danger, the sword, death or life, angles or demons, the present or the future, any powers, heights or depths, or *anything else*? No! If we are more than conquerors defined by God's love for us, which I believe we are, then each of us can say with confidence, I will fear *no* evil.

Enough said.

## Some Practical Advice

Before we conclude this chapter, dealing with fearing no evil and exercising courage in the face of it, let me leave you with just three words of practical advice. To start, it is important to pay close attention to the metaphors you use to describe evil. Do your metaphors in any way let you off the hook or absolve you from personal responsibility to deal with the evil you recognize? Do they make you an innocent but helpless victim? Remember, these metaphors will shape you every bit as much as the metaphors you use to describe your experience with God.

Also, if exercising courage in the face of evil seems like a daunting task, remember to start small—in your own neighborhood. God is not calling you to change the entire world, something that has only happened two or three times in the history of the planet. No, exercise courage in small ways right where you live. God will honor your courage, and it will shape and form you as it is exercised. Ask God to give you eyes to see and courage to speak up when you do. That's a good place to start.

Finally, if you struggle to exercise courage in the face of evil, look for role models. Spend time with those who do and learn from them. We are shaped by the relationships we nurture, so spend time with those who live like you would like to live. Good things will happen. As it turns out, both courage and kindness are contagious.

## Conclusion

Evil is a difficult topic for most of us and dealing with it is even harder. In this chapter, we started by admitting that evil is an elusive rascal, not easy to explain or describe. We looked at some metaphors in common use to describe evil and cautioned against thinking of evil in ways that remove us from any personal responsibility for facing it squarely. The place to start, it turns out, is in our own spiritual closets, dealing with the things that we have stowed away and would rather forget. The truth is, they don't go away.

We were then cautioned about turning to spiritual "quick fixes" to combat evil, especially if such fixes divide and separate us from our neighbors. Spiritual practices should bring us together, not push others out or keep them at arm's length.

Jesus' instructions to his disciples as he sent them out proved to be insightful—have a clean heart and a clear head, be holy and wise. And we were encouraged by Paul's exhortation to the Roman church: nothing can separate us from God's love—nothing, so we are more than conquerors. We need fear no evil.

Three words of practical advice were offered: (1) examine your metaphors for evil. They will shape you; (2) don't try to change or challenge the whole world. Start small, right where you live; and (3) look for role models, those who fear no evil, and spend time with them. We are shaped by the company we keep.

At the end of the day, we have to confess that fearing no evil is not an easy thing to do. Such courage does not come naturally to most of us, but it can be practiced—and it will strengthen as we do. Our prayer is that courage and kindness will stand like a stone in our lives, giving hope and dignity to those around us as we seek to be more than conquerors, faithful to the one who calls us to be holy and wise.

## Questions for Reflection and Discussion:

1. What metaphors come to mind when you think of evil? Could there be others?
2. Are there ways that you have tried to deny or ignore evil around you or in you? Are there things hidden away in your spiritual closet? What would be a good first step to clean it out?
3. How might you start in small ways to practice courage in your daily life, in your own neighborhood?
4. Who would be a good spiritual role model or mentor for you, and how might you spend more time with that person? Hint: lunch or coffee is a good way to start.

5. Many have pointed out that courage and kindness have deep spiritual connections. Why do you think this is so?

## Psalm 23

The Lord is my shepherd; I shall not want.

He makes me lie down in green pastures; He leads me beside still waters.

He restores my soul; He leads me in paths of righteousness for His name's sake.

Even though I walk through the valley of the shadow of death, I will fear no evil . . .

# CHAPTER 9

## *For You Are With Me—Companionship*

> And as ridiculous as it may sound, sometimes all any of us needs in life is for someone to hold our hand and walk next to us.
>
> —JAMES FREY

### Introduction

In Part II, we have been meditating on the metaphor of God as the gentle guide. Thus far, we have considered guidance (chapter 6), the journey called life (chapter 7), and courage in the face of evil (chapter 8). Now, we turn to companionship (*for you are with me*) before ending Part II with an exploration of how traveling with a gentle guide brings contentment, sometimes in the form of protection and sometimes in the form of correction. As it turns out, we need both along the way.

### Three Companions

Before we reflect on the companionship of the gentle guide in our lives and the spiritual consequences of a few uninvited companions, let me tell you about three companions that saved me—spiritually and professionally. I don't know about you, but when I am on my own, alone, weekends are the hardest. I guess that during the week, there are enough activities, appointments, lunches, meetings, and projects to keep my mind occupied and my heart distracted, but everything slows down on the weekend.

Uninvited thoughts and feelings creep in, and the nights can be very, very lonely. I experienced this phenomenon full force while working in San Diego. Going through a divorce, even under the best of conditions, if there is such a thing as the best of conditions, is painful to say the least, and particularly so in a conservative Christian community. Honestly, my constant companions were guilt, shame, and fear—uninvited companions who whispered in my ear in the dark of the night: you are not worthy, you are not trustworthy, and you are no longer welcome here. I carried and nurtured these feelings of inadequacy like a newborn baby.

Seeking some sense of direction and solace and reassurance, I sought out the counsel of a senior pastor at the church where I attended. He was quite familiar with both the denomination and the politics of the university. I asked him directly, "Should I resign and simply go away?" "No," he answered cautiously, and then added, "not yet." Not yet! Wow, that was not what I was hoping to hear. Not yet. If the pastor was trying to comfort and reassure me, he failed miserably. All I took away from the conversation was that the clock was ticking, and I was a problem that needed to go away—if not today, then soon. I was damaged goods, as someone told me, and an embarrassment to the university. Looking back, perhaps the pastor did not intend to communicate all of that, but that's what rattled around in my head in the middle of the night. I started looking for another place to work. I even considered driving an over-the-road truck. I guess the idea of heading out on my own in an eighteen-wheeler through the deep South with a good sound system seemed better than being asked to resign in disgrace. I wasn't too sure that I could take any more rejection.

Then out of the blue, three of my friends stepped forward and each volunteered to be my companion—committed to helping me make it through the long and lonely weekends ahead. I don't think they colluded, but each one took a specific block of the weekend. The first companion simply wouldn't let me attend church on my own. When you are suffering and down for any reason, attending church on your own is very difficult. On several occasions, I would come to the side entry of the sanctuary, look in, and simply turn around and go home. At other times, I would slip in and sit by myself. That was even worse. However, my friend would not let me stay away. He would insist that I come to church, sit with his family, and then come over for Sunday lunch before joining the family in some rousing table games. From time to time, I would purposely cheat just a bit, doing so obviously so that his children would see what

I was doing. They loved to catch me and call out my transgressions. We would all have a big laugh, I would promise to learn the rules, and then we would turn back to the game at hand. I don't think I won even a game, but I was the true winner. To this day, I have fond memories of Sunday afternoons, especially during those lonely times.

The second friend became my Saturday companion. Sometimes we would hike, or attend a sporting event, or go to Home Depot, or just hang out at home with his family. I became quite good at helping to mow the lawn, trim the trees, and even repair a fence post or two. I simply joined in with whatever his family was doing that day, and it was life-giving. And he would ask me how I was doing, and he meant it. On one occasion, I admitted that I was having trouble going through my days being sure that I didn't act *too* happy. After all, I was damaged goods, and I wasn't permitted to be joyful, a sure sign that I didn't understand the gravity of my situation. He stared at me for a minute, and then cleared his throat and asked, "Has anyone given you permission to look to the future with anticipation, even joy?" Of course, my answer was "no." "Well, I do!" he barked as he gave me an even longer and more intense stare. I received the message loud and clear. As I look back, that was a turning point for me. I started looking ahead, albeit self-consciously, to better days, and in due time they did come.

My third friend took the Friday night shift. Even though he was working two jobs and had teenage children, he told me that he was committed to spending each Friday evening with me for the entire fall semester. I immediately refused, pointing out to him that he had a family of his own, but he wouldn't take no for an answer. He told me that he had already talked it over with his wife, and they both wanted him to do this. So, every Friday evening that fall we met for dinner, then went to a movie or a hockey game or just drank coffee and talked theology and church politics. And as we did, he walked with me and watched over me.

Clearly, these three companions held my hand and walked next to me. In one of the darkest times I have ever known, they were with me, affirming their hopes and dreams for me even when I didn't have any of my own. Slowly, steadily, and surely, my spirit and joy returned. Honestly, it was a long and difficult journey, a dark season, but I made it—with the love and care of three companions. There isn't a day that goes by that I don't think about their care for me, and I pray for opportunities to do the same for other suffering souls. As it turns out, they are everywhere, *and as ridiculous as it may sound, sometimes all any of us needs in life is for someone to hold our hand and walk next to us.* Lord, let it be me. Amen.

## Uninvited Companions

Before we examine the positive and formative role that companionship plays in our lives and the loving work of the gentle guide as we make our way home, we need to acknowledge that at times we travel with some uninvited companions—hitchhikers that drain away our emotional and spiritual energy as we carry them, for they will not carry their own weight. We do all the heavy lifting.

Let me name some common culprits: doubts, fears, guilt, and shame. From time to time, we all entertain some doubts and fears. This, in and of itself, is not a serious problem. In many respects, it is part of life, but sometimes they beg questions that take us deep and far beyond worry about a job or keeping our reputation intact. I call them existential concerns. They are real. They are serious, and they will join us on our journeys at the most unexpected times. It is not that we worry that we have failed at something (which we all do at one time or another), but that *we are a failure*. It is not that we fear that our work is unimportant, but that *we are insignificant*. It isn't that we have doubts that we will be remembered, but that *we have nothing to be remembered for*. It isn't that we worry about death, but that *we have never lived*. These are not doubts that we can readily or comfortably address, but our lives ask these questions of us and beg for answers, and if they are not acknowledged and resolved, such uninvited companions can travel with us for a lifetime, leading us down some unnecessary and unhealthy paths.

Two other uninvited companions need to be mentioned—guilt and shame. Guilt is an internal feeling that you have done something wrong, and shame is the persistent feeling that something is wrong with you. Of course, at times we do things that cause (or should cause) us to feel guilt. This is normal, and it is a healthy response to actions and attitudes that hurt and marginalize others. At one time or another, most of us have spoken unkindly to the persons we love most in this world. Why we do so, I do not know, but we do. When this happens, we feel a sense of guilt and try as best we can to ask for forgiveness and make amends. This is healthy, but when the guilt and regret remain alive and active years after apologies have been accepted and forgiveness has been extended, it becomes unnecessary baggage. Often, it is the result of not being willing or able to forgive ourselves. Shedding such guilt is one of the hardest things we will ever do, but we must if we are to journey lightly and make our way home.

Shame, guilt's first cousin, is thicker, tougher, and stickier to deal with. It is the sense that something is terribly wrong with us—that we are damaged goods. I can still hear my father raise his voice and say to me, "Shame on you! What's the matter with you!" after being caught using some of his forbidden tools in the garage. Really, I think he meant that I should feel some sense of guilt for what I had done, and I did, and he applied a bit of homegrown disciplinary discomfort to make his point. But some of us journey through life with a deep sense that we are profoundly flawed, and we fear that someone will shout, "Shame on you! What's the matter with you!" and point us out to everyone we know and care about. And when we are exposed, we will never recover; all will be lost. Such a burden is terribly difficult to carry, and heavy, too.

So, how do we constructively deal with existential doubts and fears, guilt, and shame? I doubt that there is a universal answer to this question, and certainly not a simply one. We all must make our own way, but that doesn't mean that we are left to our own wits. In what follows, we will look first at the accrued benefits of companionship that provide perspective, trust, confidence, and hope, and then celebrate the character of the gentle guide who is after us, with us, and in us. This is good news for any traveler, and that is all of us.

## Accrued Benefits of Companionship

There are certain things in life that cannot adequately be explained; they have to be experienced to be fully understood. I believe that companionship is on that list. When we have a companion or a small group of companions who share life together, what accrues over time from all the things we face together—the good, bad, and ugly—are memories. And memories are the vital soil from which perspective, trust, confidence, and hope germinate and flourish.

Memories open a window to view the past. Over time, they merge together and provide a rich narrative of good and not so good times, of celebrations and tears, and of triumphs and failures. Memories offer a glimpse—not of perfection, but of persistence; not of sainthood, but of humble and honest efforts. With such a perspective of life—not as perfect, but ultimately real and good—comes a sense of trust in the journey. Companions have walked with us in the toughest of times, and we made it. We are still here. They were there for us in the darkest of times, and they will be there with us even now, wherever there is. We can look to the future with confidence and a hope that is real, for we have experienced what cannot be explained—the gift of traveling companions who held our hand and walked next to us, come what may.

## The Gentle Guide

Most of us are familiar with the old saying, "blood is thicker than water," meaning that the bonds of family are powerful, stronger than friendships. Yet we read in Proverbs, "there is a friend who sticks closer than a brother" (18:24b). Closer than a brother? Really? Yes, really. It is God, the Holy Spirit, the gentle guide. I have come to believe that the companionship of the gentle guide is so powerful because it plays out in three distinct ways in our spiritual journeys.

### *After Us*

First, the gentle guide pursues us. The Quakers are fond of saying that "there is that of God in everyone," a spark the gives God access, a holy tug, and we see in the story of the prodigal son that while he was still a long way off, the father saw him, had compassion for him, and came running (Luke 15:20). It is a wonderful image of God—running after us, running to us, while we are still a long way off, which is all of us at one time or another. I sincerely believe that the gentle guide is eager to be our companion—to embrace us and show us the way, calling out to us and providing a sense of the right paths to follow in ways known and unknown. The gentle guide is after us long before we are aware that we are in need of direction and spiritual companionship.

### *With Us*

As we become more intentional about our spiritual journeys, it is clear that the gentle guide is not only with us, but as we look back we can see the fingerprints of the gentle guide all over our lives. I think about decisions I made because of a vague sense that it was the right way to go or thing to do, like going off to college and heading to seminary right after college. Even though at the time it seemed to be a dead end for me, that path opened up relationships and opportunities that set my entire career in Christian higher education in motion. Who knew? You can say what you will, but I truly believe that it was the work of the gentle guide, who was at work in my life in ways that I did not fully know or understand. And because of the companionship of the gentle guide, I have every reason to believe that wherever I go, when I get there, wherever there is, the gentle guide is already there and working on my behalf. The gentle guide is not only after us, but with us.

## *In Us*

We are truly thankful for the ways the gentle guide directs our lives, ways known and unknown, but perhaps the most profound work of the gentle guide is not direction, but instruction. Of course, if we are on a wilderness trek, we would listen and follow the instructions of the trail guide—take this trail, stop and rest here, drink some water, don't camp in that low place, avoid the poison ivy, and so on. The trail guide directs our movements because we are novices, and we would be in trouble if left to our own wits. But along the way, the trail guide has the opportunity to not only lead, but to teach us as well. Here is the correct way to tie your boots, carry your pack, build a fire, forage off the land, hydrate, set up a camp site, rest, care for fellow travelers, and enjoy the journey. And as the trail guide teaches us, we become better, more experienced travelers, able to not only journey on our own, but to instruct and care for other less experienced travelers, too.

I have come to believe that the gentle guide works in much the same way for us as we make our spiritual journey toward home. To be sure, we receive direction that keeps us from wrong turns, danger, and harm, but the gentle guide is also the ever-present teacher, instructing us and enabling us to journey with wisdom, grace, and understanding, able to make our way with confidence and perspective and hope, and able to help other travelers to make their way.

At the end of the day, God can never be fully explained, only experienced, and we are thankful for the companionship of the gentle guide. We are pursued before we are even aware of any need for a companion. The gentle guide travels with us, both directing our paths and teaching us as we mature as travelers to wisely hear and follow the gentle guide's voice and make our way with perspective, trust, and confidence. And as we do, we come alongside others as they make their way home, gladly traveling with them and sharing what we have learned from the gentle guide, who is lovingly after us, with us, and working in us.

## Scripture

When we think about companionship, it is difficult to think of a better example than the story of Ruth, found in the Old Testament book by the same name. It is a story familiar to many of us, often told, at least in part, in Sunday school or Vacation Bible School. It is a beautiful story of loyalty and faithfulness with an interesting twist at the end.

Because of a famine in the land, an Israelite family from Bethlehem was forced to move to Moab to find food and work. Shortly after arrival, the father died, and later the two sons, both married by then to Moabite women, also died, leaving their mother (Naomi) and the two daughters-in-law (Ruth and Orpah) to fend for themselves. Naomi decided that she needed to return to her own country and urged Orpah and Ruth to leave her and return to their own families. It was obvious that they loved each other, so the decision was excruciating for them all. Finally, Orpah decided to go back to her family, but Ruth would not hear of it, declaring, "Don't urge me to leave you or to turn back from you. Where you go I will go, and where you stay I will stay. Your people will be my people and your God my God" (Ruth 1:16).

So Naomi and Ruth returned to Bethlehem. There, Ruth met Boaz while gleaning in the wheat and barley fields. They were subsequently married, and Ruth gave birth to a son. This, of course, was almost more than Naomi, who had lost her husband and both sons, could imagine. She would help raise her grandson. What a perfect ending to a sad and difficult journey.

But wait, there is more. Ruth's baby boy, Obed, was the father of Jesse, who was the father of David the King (4:13–17). So, Ruth is King David's great-grandmother, as listed in the genealogy of Jesus in the first chapter of the Gospel of Matthew (v. 5). It's an ending to the story that even Disney couldn't imagine!

I think that there are two takeaways from the story of Naomi and Ruth germane to this meditation on companionship. First, we all need people in our lives who will say in effect, "Where you go I will go . . . Your people will be my people . . ." In other words, "I am in—totally in through thick and thin. You can count on me." I must confess that such companions are few and far between, and they are a gift. Count such companions as grace upon grace, and strive to be such a person to others. It isn't always easy to journey with others, but it is a way we give back for all we have received along the way.

Second, every decision has its own moral trajectory. That is, the decisions we make take us somewhere, but we rarely know at the time where that somewhere will be. In this story, Ruth's decision to be Naomi's companion through thick and thin gave Naomi a sense of hope and landed Ruth in the genealogy of Jesus as the great-grandmother of David the King. Who could have imagined! No one—and that's just the point. Not every story, of course, will have a Hollywood ending. That's not the promise. But we do know this: we are called to be faithful; God will do the heavy lifting. We are asked to live in the present, to be present; God knows the paths we will travel. We can trust the gentle guide.

## Some Practical Advice

Before we conclude this chapter, let me offer several words of practical advice as we all try to make our way home, led by the gentle guide. First, set aside some time and reflect back on your own spiritual journey. Remember those times when someone walked with you and held your hand. Give thanks for these experiences and memories that bring perspective, courage, and hope as you look ahead, knowing that you have never been alone.

Be grateful for faithful friends. They are truly a gift from God. Find a way to say "thank you," and reflect on your shared experiences. Be personal. Think of what makes them smile—some homemade cookies, a coffee, a walk, a round of golf, or an outdoor concert—to mention just a few. Let them know how much their companionship has meant to you, and always will. Take time to invest in their lives, too.

Finally, if someone has been a companion to you, and that is most of us, pay it forward. Find someone in need of companionship and walk with them as others have walked with you. It is the best way I know to honor those who have journeyed with us and cared about us. Share your own story of the faithfulness of the gentle guide in your spiritual journey.

It will encourage them, and remind you that companionship is a free gift—but priceless.

## Conclusion

This chapter began with a personal story of three companions who walked with me and held my hand as I journeyed through a very difficult season in my life, providing a glimpse into what ideas and advice would follow in this meditation. We acknowledged that some uninvited companions can accompany us as we travel. They add extra weight and slow us down—doubts, fears, guilt, and shame. And they rarely just go away on their own, so dealing with them honestly and intentionally is the order of the day. For most of us, this is a communal task, better in the loving care of faithful companions than wrestling with them on our own.

The two primary themes of the meditation dealt first with memories of the journey that bring perspective and yield trust, confidence, and hope, and then the companionship of the gentle guide who is after us, with us, and working in us. From Scripture, the story of Ruth provided a stunning example of companionship under the most difficult of situations, and then offered an equally stunning insight that more often than not, there is a trajectory to our actions that takes us to unexpected and unimagined places. As it turns out, Ruth is cited by Matthew in the genealogy of Jesus (1:5). Who could have dreamed of such an ending!

To conclude this chapter, three words of practical advice were offered: (1) take time to think back on your own journey and be grateful for the companionship of friends and the gentle guide, (2) be sure to express your appreciation to those who have walked with you in intentional and personal ways, and (3) look for opportunities to be a companion to other suffering souls, thus "paying it forward," one of the most practical and meaningful spiritual disciplines we can undertake.

At the end of the day, we are all on a journey, and we have to admit that although we often want to travel alone or at least try to deal with whatever we face on our own, the gentle guide is always with us, pursuing us, holding our hand and walking with us (often in the form of faithful companions), and working within us, too, as we make our way home. Thanks be to God.

## Questions for Reflection and Discussion:

1. What is your story of someone walking with you and holding your hand as you journeyed through a difficult season in your life? Have you shared it recently? Might you pray for direction about how to share your story with someone who is struggling right now?
2. Which uninvited companions do you carry: doubts, fears, guilt, or shame? Why do you think that this is so, and what might you do to deal with these uninvited companions?
3. When you think of companionship, what memories come to mind? Do they offer any perspective and confidence about how to face other difficulties that might come your way?
4. How has the gentle guide pursued you? Do you have a story to share with someone?
5. Who might you seek out and intentionally express gratitude for their companionship?

## Psalm 23

The LORD is my shepherd; I shall not want.

He makes me lie down in green pastures; He leads me beside still waters.

He restores my soul; He leads me in paths of righteousness for His name's sake.

Even though I walk through the valley of the shadow of death, I will fear no evil;

For you are with me . . .

# CHAPTER 10

## *Your Rod and Your Staff, They Comfort Me— Contentment*

> At some point, you gotta let go, and sit still,
> and allow contentment to come to you.
>
> —ELIZABETH GILBERT

### Introduction

In this chapter, we will examine the connection between "the rod—protection" and "the staff—correction," and spiritual contentment. On the face of it, such a connection may not be immediately evident, but I have come to believe that contentment requires boundaries and role models that allow us and teach us to journey safely between the rails, lacking nothing, with no empty spaces. Ultimately, contentment is a quiet, confident frame of spirit, not something we earn, but rather something we learn as we embrace the companionship of the gentle guide who works for us, in us, and through us. It is the by-product of a life well-lived, a gift, something we let come to us as we let go, sit still, and look back with gratitude to see God's constant faithfulness to us.

### Family Stories

Before we examine how protection (rod) and correction (staff) work together to provide a sense of contentment, regardless of the circumstances we face, let me begin with a few family stories that illustrate how such connections are establish and reinforced. As we shall see, we need boundaries and role models to make our way, and these are often established, for good or for ill, at home.

### Line Up!

I grew up with three brothers, one older and two younger, and a dog, in a neighborhood that was literally full of children. It was a wonderful place to spend a childhood. In the summer, we would play hide-and-seek until it was dark, and then bloody murder till we were called in for a bath, a bedtime story, then off to bed. On most days it was quite an idyllic setting. Most days, that is, but not all days. Sometimes one of us would accidentally break a window, take some of my dad's tools without permission and fail to return them (or even worse lose them), or help ourselves to the bounty of a neighbor's garden. When such events occurred, Dad would announce in a loud voice, "Line up!" The four of us would line up in age order in the living room and begin to cry. We knew what was coming. We would all receive a spanking for what transpired, and then we would be sent to our rooms to contemplate the consequences of our actions.

Once we asked Dad why we all received punishment when only one or two brothers were actually responsible for the transgression. "Good question," Dad rejoined. "You boys do so many things and don't get caught, so when I catch one of you doing something wrong, I punish all four." We thought it over for a bit and nodded our heads in agreement. Logic wasn't Dad's usual weapon of choice, but this time it all made sense. Along the way, we learned that there were consequences for our misdeeds, and sometimes what we did hurt others, too. Misbehavior, as it turns out, is really a communal act. We set things in motion that impact others. We are all connected.

### The Dodge Parking Lot

We lived in a small town and attended a small church on the main road leading to Saginaw, one located right next to the Dodge dealership. It was a convenient arrangement. The dealership was closed on Sundays, so the church made use of their parking lot. My dad made use of their parking lot, too. If one of us acted out in church, my dad would unceremoniously remove the offending party from the sanctuary, take him out to the parking lot, and apply some "medicine."

I remember in particular one occasion when my grandmother felt "the blessing" and began walking around the sanctuary, waving a white handkerchief and letting out a whoop or two. My brother and I thought that she was having too much fun to be left to herself, so we decided to join her. We got out our handkerchiefs, waved them in the air, and walked around the sanctuary following grandma. Following grandma, that is, until our dad caught us in mid-stride, and out to the Dodge parking lot we went for another round of medicine.

To this day, I am still a bit nervous about driving a Dodge, and I'm fearful of showing too much emotion in church. If I raise my hands during worship, which I do very rarely, I do so with a funny feeling that someone is approaching me from behind. On a more serious note, the trip to the Dodge parking lot taught me several important guiding principles: (1) never make fun of anyone's heartfelt religious expressions, no matter how unusual they may seem to you; and (2) don't ever put on a religious act for the amusement of others or in an attempt to edify yourself. Be real, be honest, and be sincere about what you believe, what you feel, and how you worship. Over the years, these hard-learned principles have served me well.

## School Days

My older brother is just fourteen months older than me. When I started grade school, I looked up to him. Until well into high school, I wore his hand-me-down cloths, and I did so with pride. He was a model for me in more ways that he will ever know. We attended the same elementary school, Michigan Avenue School, and he always looked out for me—usually from a distance. From the start, we had our own circle of friends. It wasn't something we ever talked about, but I instinctively knew to keep my distance during recess and play with my own classmates. Looking back, it was really a healthy arrangement, giving each of us our own social space, something that was certainly in short supply since we shared a bedroom where we slept, along with the dog, in bunk beds. And we had one bathroom for a family of six. Privacy was at a premium.

So, I made my own way in school, but I always looked at what my brother had done and was doing for guidance. And if a bully started to pick on me or one of my friends, my brother would suddenly be standing right behind me, saying "Why don't you pick on someone your own size?" That would bring the confrontation to a sudden and satisfactory end, and life on the playground would return to normal. To this day, I don't know how he could have been so engrossed in whatever activity he was involved in with his friends, yet always had an eye out for me. I suspect that my mother told him to look out for me, in much the same way she told me to look after my younger brothers, which I did faithfully. After all, we were family.

On an occasion or two, my friends and I would start teasing someone from our class, taking her hat or hiding his coat on the playground. Mysteriously, my brother would appear just behind us and say, "That's enough of that. We don't treat people that way. We treat people like we would like to be treated." And then looking directly at me, he would continue, "Do you want to be treated that way?" The answer was obvious. I shook my head and stared at the ground, embarrassed that I had crossed an invisible and unspoken line. As it turns out, my older brother offered both protection and correction, and at different times, both were needed—the rod and the staff. Looking back now, I appreciate his interventions, even when I was called to account. His protection gave me a sense that I was not left on my own, and his correction made it clear that I was to be kind, too. I was to treat others in the way that I would want to be treated, a lesson that I have tried to follow throughout my professional life. In fact, I have come to believe that kindness is the soil in which all the other virtues grow and thrive. I don't know if my brother would have expressed it that way in the third grade, but his actions surely did.

*Cinnamon Graham Crackers*

Perhaps the greatest lesson I learned in grade school came on a mid-fall morning during my first year in school—in kindergarten. Back in the day, we took a small rug to kindergarten to use during nap time, and after our quiet time, we would have a half-pint of milk and a snack supplied in turn by a student. When it was my turn to take a snack to school, I asked my older brother for advice. Without hesitation he said, "Take cinnamon graham crackers. Everyone loves them, even the girls." So, my mother took me down to the local grocery store and we bought a box of crackers (actually she supplied the funds, but I gave the cashier the money and kept the change).

Honestly, I was very excited to go to school the next day, knowing that I would take my place among the kindergarten social elite, such as it was in our small town. It was during the nap time that it hit me—I had forgotten to bring the crackers to school, leaving them on the kitchen table. Panic set in. Cell phones and email hadn't been invented yet, so I knew of no way to contact my mom. I just sat at my desk with a sick feeling in the pit of my stomach, knowing that instead of taking my place among the social elite, I would now be a social outcast, exposed as an irresponsible classmate, having let the entire class down during snack time.

Just then, there was a knock at the door. My teacher called to me and said that there was someone there to see me. As I approached the door, I could see that it was my mother, and she was holding the box of cinnamon graham crackers! I sank to my knees and hugged mother around hers, overjoyed that the disaster of all disasters had been averted. She smiled sweetly and said to me, "Your brother remembered what you had forgotten, asked to be excused from his class to go to the principal's office, and called me—and here I am. Don't ever forget, Patrick, you can count on me, and you can count on your brother." And you know what? She was right.

### Don't Forget Where You Came From

When I was ready to go off to college, leaving each of my younger brothers with their own bedroom, it was a rather unceremonious event. The younger brother who was to inherit my bedroom (which I had to myself for almost a year) knocked on the door at 6:00 AM and stood there with a box of his personal items, asking if I had moved out yet. Actually, I smiled, knowing what it was to have even a little space to call your own. I told him that I would be out by 8:00, and I was, and he joyfully moved in, waving goodbye and wishing me good luck at college as he was putting his things in the dresser drawers.

My parents drove the 120 miles to college in a station wagon and deposited my belongings on the sidewalk in front of my dorm. My room was on the fourth floor and there were no elevators, so my parents decided that it would be good for me to carry everything up myself. "It will build character," was my father's favorite line. We said our good-byes right there on the sidewalk. Just before they pulled away, my father leaned out the car window and said, "You're an Allen. Don't forget where you came from." I nodded in agreement and waved. I watched our car until it was out of sight, and then started carrying the boxes up to my room. My character formation had begun.

Being an Allen meant that I was responsible for more than just myself. I represented a family, my people, so what I did was a reflection of them, too. My father wanted to be sure that I conducted myself in a way that would make the entire family proud, and I could return home with my head held high. From time to time when I returned home, someone would ask me, "You're an Allen, aren't you?" And I would reply with pride, "I sure am—always will be."

And I have never forgotten where I came from. I grew up in a small town with good neighbors, caring teachers, a formative church, and a loving family. I have had the good fortune to travel around the world, working at some very fine Christian universities, and even publish a book or two, but I have never forgotten the profound values that I was taught (and caught) there—your word is your bond, there is honor in hard work, everyone deserves your respect, you love God by loving your neighbor, and kindness is never an option. "Don't forget where you came from." That's good advice for all of us.

* * *

I trust these childhood stories will serve as a reminder that we all come from somewhere, and even in the most insignificant events, as we look back, we can see God's fingerprints all over our lives, offering protection and correction, often through the care of those who love us, and even some who don't. In what follows, we will examine both the rod (protection) and the staff (correction) mentioned in Psalm 23, and I will make the case that the rod and staff provide us with boundaries and role models who direct us as we journey toward home with the gentle guide. And on the journey, we begin to develop a sense of contentment, a gracious gift that comes to us as we travel, the knowledge that our life is full, not perfect but complete, and we can trust the gentle guide.

## Your Rod—Protection

In chapter 1, we discussed the work of the good shepherd as a protector at length and suggested that the good shepherd not only protects us *from* certain events, disappointments, and difficulties but also protects us *for* future things as well, although such protection is often only recognized while reflecting later on our lives, if it is recognized at all. I have learned to pray, "God, we pause to thank you for the many blessings in our lives—known and unknown, remembered and forgotten." I believe that there are more than we can possibly imagine, let alone recognize and remember. For them all, I am thankful.

The gentle guide, the organizing metaphor of Part II, also offers us protection as we make our way. After all, the gentle guide has already been where we are trying to go, knows the way, and knows that real danger can come our way. Not everyone will have our best interests at heart and not everything is good for us, even if the path looks safe and inviting at the time. When Jesus sent out his disciples, warning them that they would be like sheep among wolves (Matt 10:16), it went without saying that there would be wolves in sheep's clothing, too. The disciples were to be shrewd—wise, discerning, insightful, and smart as they traveled. That's good advice for all of us.

Sometimes the paths ahead look exciting and inviting, but we are met with a closed door—a rejection letter on a book proposal, someone else is hired for the job we wanted so badly, or a business decides "to go another way," leaving our hopes and dreams in pieces and our plans out in the cold. Sometimes, we fervently pray but there is no answer, or the answer we receive is a "no." Honestly, these are disappointing and painful times, and it is OK to say so. God can take it; lament is always welcome in God's care. However, looking back, I can see so many times when what I wanted to do would have been a dead end, the wrong place at the wrong time, or just plain awful. Sometimes we see the gentle guide use the rod to chase away the wolves from the door, but more often than not, we are unaware of the wisdom, care, and protection that shield us from so many difficulties, not the least of which come from our own sense of privilege and pride that push us to follow our own instincts and desires rather than depending on the care and direction from the one who walks with us and loves us more than we could ever imagine.

## Your Staff—Correction

The gentle guide not only offers protection from difficulties seen and unseen, known and unknown, but correction, too. It is by both the rod (protection) and the staff (correction) that we are guided to safety. Remember, the rod is used to fend away that which comes to harm us, external threats, while the staff is used to pull us out of dangerous and unhealthy situations and places where we have no business being in the first place. The crook on the staff is intended for our own necks, to pull us away from the thicket and back to safety. While such correction is not always pleasant, it is certainly necessary, particularly given our bent to push the boundaries and go to unwise places and get into ill-advised situations. As Paul wrote, "I do not understand what I do. For what I want to do I do not do, but what I hate I do" (Rom 7:15). In other words, we know better, but we do it anyway. This comes as no surprise to the gentle guide, who carries both a rod and a staff for good reason.

Wouldn't it be nice if we had a built-in GPS system that would keep us on the right path, and if we strayed and wandered off the path, it would simply announce, "Recalculating, recalculating," and then new directions would be given without condemnation, anger, or frustration; just new directions? It certainly would be nice, but that's not the way life works. Thankfully, however, we are not left to our own wits. Our gentle guide directs our paths in numerous ways but let me name three in particular that often escape recognition—fence posts, guide posts, and lamp posts.

### *Fence Posts*

If you have ever had the joy of walking or hunting in a deciduous forest just after the leaves fall and before the snow flies, you will note that the wire fences running through the woods are almost invisible, but not so the fence posts. Most metal ones have a painted white top, and they are easy to spot since the white color and their verticality seem out of place in the underbrush and quickly catch the eye. Those white tips have saved me more than once from walking full steam into a fence while hunting. They served as an early warning system of sorts, signaling to me to take care and watch where I was going. All was not as it seemed to be.

And fence posts also support the fence that marks out a plot of land or territory. A study of children playing next to a busy street found that they only used 60 percent of the playground. As you might expect, they were constantly being warned to "stay out of the street" and "don't play near the street," and they followed instructions. They did their best to obey, which was most difficult, especially when a ball rolled into the middle of the street. The school decided to fence off the playground from the highway. Now the children could play right up next to the fence without fear, and they could even use the fence as a backstop in some of their games. As a result, 100 percent of the playground was used as intended. The fence provided protection, a safe perimeter, and a boundary that marked out safe territory.

I think that all of us need spiritual fences as we make our way. We need boundaries to let us know where it is safe to go and where we need to take caution. We all know of good people who "crossed the line" of one kind or another, and they (and their families) paid a huge price. There were no fences, or they chose to ignore the fence posts, and they ended up in the middle of the sad and unsafe highway or deep in a thicket of their own doing. Close friends and family can serve as fence posts, just as when my older brother challenged me, "You're an Allen. We don't treat people that way." To this day, this understanding serves as a boundary for me. I just won't go there.

And sometimes we need correction in the form of accountability—friends, the wisdom of Scripture, experience, and that still small voice that calls us out and calls out to us to pay attention, that we are headed straight into the underbrush at full speed. We all need to establish and maintain spiritual fences for protection *and* correction. The good news is that as we journey, we need not travel alone; there is safety in numbers. Spiritual fences are simply a form of grace upon grace, helping us see what dangers wait ahead when we stray off the path or lose our sense of true north and deliberately choose to go our own way. They also show us where to play, using all that is available to us. It seems to me that the time to check our spiritual fences is long before we really need them. Let's do so today.

## Guide Posts

While fence posts create boundaries for safe travel and correction when we are headed toward danger, guide posts let us know that we are on the right path and show us the way to go. Some guide posts even tell us how much farther it is to the next fork in the road, always a decision point.

When we are hiking on an unfamiliar path in unfamiliar surroundings, a guide post is such a welcome sight. It says in effect, "welcome, you're doing fine; you're on the right path and here's the way forward." When you come to a guide post, there is reassurance, knowing that someone has been here before, wherever "here" is, and you can make your way, too. Someone has marked the way for you.

When I think of spiritual guide posts, I think of role models—individuals in my life who have been where I want to go, who demonstrate how to live faithfully in this world, and how to prepare for the journey to the next with confidence, courage, and contentment. I have come to believe that having and heeding the spiritual guide posts in our lives are two of the most important aspects of the Christian life, whether we are new to the faith or seasoned travelers. Fence posts mark out the safe territory, and guide posts assure us of the right path and point the way forward. Both are priceless.

*Lamp Posts*

One final post bears mentioning—a lamp post. There is nothing more comforting to the traveler than to see that the lights are on and someone is home. Coming out of the woods after dark or making your way in a terrible storm, just a glimpse of a lamp post or a light in the window brings comfort. You know you're almost home. Sometimes in the middle of a very dark time or place, it is the only thing in life that you can point to and count on. Even the smallest of candles can dispel a great deal of darkness.

And there are spiritual lamp posts that point the way home. There are the testimonies of those who have traveled the road before us, a veritable cloud of witnesses. There is the faithful companionship of friends, family, mentors, and role models who walk with us and encourage us as we journey. There are the promises found in Scripture, such as the words of Jesus: "I go to prepare a place for you" (John 14:2b, TSK), and there is the still small voice in the middle of night that brings assurance, "I am with you, follow my voice, I will gently guide you." Look and be thankful for the lamp posts in your life and travel safely. The lights are always on, showing the way, and welcoming us home. Thanks be to God!

## Contentment

As I suggested in the opening paragraphs of this chapter, contentment is a quiet, confident, inward frame of spirit, something that comes to us as we sit still and remember our journeys and the work of the gentle guide along the way. We remember times of protection and correction when the rod and the staff were applied, often due to our own stubborn insistence that we knew where we were going and could travel on our own. In doing so, we lost our way and ended up in a thicket or a dead end or worse. We remember fence posts, guide posts, and lamp posts that offered boundaries and role models for us as we made our way, not perfectly, but faithfully. They gave us an inner sense of true north, that we were in a good place, doing the right things. And we remember the companionship of the gentle guide who worked for us, in us, and through us, giving our lives consequence and purpose. As we look back in gratitude, we see that we were never alone, even though at times we thought we were, and acted like we were, too.

The clearest expression of contentment I know comes to us from the writings of the Apostle Paul: "I have learned the secret of being content in any and every situation, whether well fed or hungry, whether living in plenty or in want. I can do all things through him who gives me strength" (Phil 4:12b–13). In any and every situation, well fed or hungry, in plenty or in want—that is both powerful and instructive, particularly so since Paul was in chains in prison when he penned these words. It was not the best of times for him, to say the least. Yet he was content because he remembered his journey and the rod and staff of the gentle guide, and Paul certainly needed both from time to time. He was content because he had learned that contentment comes from a relationship—*through him* who gives me strength, and I would add protection, correction, boundaries, and role models. Paul could say that he was (spiritually) in a good place, doing the right things, and he was content in his rich relationship with the gentle guide.

There is a subtle shift in Psalm 23 that indicates such a growing relationship with God, too, from a description of God at arm's length: *he* makes me lie down, *he* leads me, *he* restores my soul—to a personal embrace of the gentle guide: *you* are with me, *your* rod, *your* staff. Such a relationship is indeed a gift of grace—unexpected, unearned, but greatly appreciated and much needed as we make our way home. When Paul pleaded with God to remove "a troubling thorn" from his flesh, God's word to him was, "My grace is sufficient for you" (2 Cor 12:9). As we journey, may we remember and be content in knowing that God's grace has been sufficient for each of us, and always will be, for *your* rod and *your* staff, they comfort us.

## Scripture

In one of the most tender exchanges found in all of Scripture, Jesus predicts his betrayal and offers comfort to his disciples by telling them that although he is going away, he will be back to take them there, too, and then adds, "You know the way to the place where I am going" (John 14:4). Thomas, who was never shy about sharing what he was thinking, even his doubts and concerns, leaned in and asked Jesus what most of the disciples were probably thinking, "Lord, we don't know where you are going, so how can we know the way?" (14:5). Good question—honest question. Jesus answered, "I am the way" (14:6a).

All of us who claim Christ affirm that Jesus is the way, but at the same time most of us have some doubts from time to time, too—how can we know the way? If the disciples who walked with Jesus, sat under his teaching, and saw his miracles had doubts, we don't need to beat ourselves up for having a doubt or two ourselves. While we know that Jesus is the way, we need some fence posts, guide posts, and lamp posts to help us find our way home. Thankfully, we are not left to our own wits.

The Apostle Paul offers us some assistance as we look to be faithful Christ followers. "Follow my example, as I follow the example of Christ" (1 Cor 11:1). Just as we see the Father through the life of Jesus, we see Jesus through the lives of those who follow him. Paul simply declares, follow my example. What a bold statement, something that fits well with what we know of Paul. If he was anything, he was certainly unflinching when it came to his faith in Christ. I wonder if we would have the confidence in our faith to tell those who walk with us, follow me as I follow Christ? That's a spiritual practice that is worth considering.

And Paul doubles down on his offer to be a role model in his Letter to the Philippians: "Whatever you have learned or received or heard from me, or seen in me—put it into practice. And the God of peace will be with you" (4:9). Here Paul offers several ways that we can gain insight and direction, certainly from him, but also from those who serve as mentors and role models in our own lives. We can receive instruction, direction, protection, and correction. The key, it seems to me, is to put into practice that which has been taught to us and modeled for us. And as we do, we find that the peace of God is with us, that contentment has found us.

## Some Practical Advice

Before we close this meditation on contentment, let me offer just a few words of practical advice. At one time or another and in one way or another, we are all a bit like Thomas, so much wanting to know the way but struggling to find and stay on the path. And if we are honest, there are times that we just want to lean in and say to Jesus, "If we're not sure where we are going, how can we know the way?" Fair question. Honest question. Hopefully, the following will be helpful.

### Embrace Doubt

Don't be afraid to be like Thomas. If you have doubts, and all of us do from time to time, lean in and express them, and if you have questions, ask! Surely the God of the universe will not be disturbed or frightened by a few doubts or questions. God can take it. In fact, I believe that God longs for honest interaction with us, so bring your doubts and fears and be real. Embrace your doubts—I know that God will, too.

### Pay Attention

Intentionally set aside some time to reflect on the guidance you have received in your life and what is at your disposal right now—the fence posts, guide posts, and lamp posts that provide both boundaries and direction as you make your way. What boundaries have you established that keep you from losing your way, and is it possible that you are outside the lines or off the path right now? What course adjustments do you need to make? What would be the first step?

If you're in the dark, feeling lost and very much alone, what lamp posts do you have, or could you have, in your life? Who is providing you with light for the journey home and showing you the way? Who speaks into your life? And is it possible that you might be a gentle guide or role model for someone close to you? After all, no one need travel alone. Ask God to show you the work of the gentle guide in your own life and ask to be shown how you might be a role model for someone else. Then, it's a matter of keeping your eyes and ears open. Opportunities will come to you and for you. Just lean in and follow.

### Accept Correction

It is easy and fun to receive praise, but correction—not so much. Yet, to be able to accept correction may be one of the most essential and beneficial spiritual disciplines we can practice. When correction comes your way, and it sometimes comes in waves, simply start by saying, "thank you," and mean it as best you can. You'll get better at it and be better for it. Correction does not mean that you are a failure, so there is no reason to deny or avoid it. Rather, receive it, hold it, consider it, even if it is painful or embarrassing at the time. Honestly, you'll get over it or past it, and as you put correction to work in your life, you will see a way forward and find your way home. As it turns out, we need both the rod and the staff from time to time. The protection and correction offered by the gentle guide comfort us, keeping us on the right path and out of the deep woods.

### Let Contentment Come

Don't put contentment on your to-do list, even though it is worth its weight in gold. Remember, we can't simply create contentment or win it on our own. No, contentment comes to us as a by-product of a life faithfully lived. As we look back on our spiritual travels, we realize the direction and companionship we have received from the gentle guide, and we are grateful for those who have walked with us, providing both boundaries and role models. And we understand that the rod and the staff were sometimes necessary to keep us from straying away from the path and into harm's way. This grateful recognition of the work of the gentle guide and those who walk with us brings a deep sense of comfort, and as we let go and sit still, contentment finds us—and it is good.

## Conclusion

In this chapter, we examined the connection between the rod (protection) and the staff (correction) and spiritual contentment. Sometimes, this connection is not all that obvious, but I believe it is there. After sharing some childhood stories that illustrated one way that behavioral and spiritual boundaries can be established, we looked at several kinds of protection at work in our lives—both protection *from* that which would harm us and protection *for* events, relationships, and activities that lie ahead. Often this kind of protection goes unnoticed and unappreciated.

We then bemoaned the fact that we do not have a built-in GPS that would tell us which way to go and recalculate our route when we lose our way. It would be nice to have such an aid, but we don't. What we do have, however, are various kinds of posts that do guide us if we pay attention—fence posts that provide safe boundaries and mark areas to avoid, guide posts to direct our paths, and lamp posts that provide comfort and direction in our darkest nights, showing us the way and bidding us home. The lights are always on.

We took counsel from the Apostle Paul who declared that he was content in *any* situation because of his relationship with Christ. At the end of the day, it is not about the circumstances we face, but rather the companions we trust. And after examining Paul's challenge to follow him as he follows Christ, several words of practical advice were offered: (1) embrace your doubts, don't deny or run from them. God can take it; (2) take time and be intentional about examining the boundaries and role models in your own spiritual journey; (3) accept correction—it's good for you, even when it hurts; and (4) don't try to manufacture contentment because you can't. It is a by-product of a life faithfully lived, so focus on having good boundaries and role models in your own life, and let your life speak to others. As you do, contentment will find you.

## Questions for Reflection and Discussion:

1. Can you think of a time when you encountered a painful disappointment only to look back and see that you were protected from a disastrous situation? Did it change your view of guidance?
2. What boundaries and values did you learn from your own family?
3. Who is the most influential role model in your spiritual life? How so?
4. Has there been a time when someone spoke directly into your life, offering correction or a warning for the path you were traveling? Have you ever done that for someone else?

5. What is the most helpful spiritual advice you have ever received? Did you ask for this advice or did it come as an unsolicited gift?

## Psalm 23

The LORD is my shepherd; I shall not want.

He makes me lie down in green pastures; He leads me beside still waters.

He restores my soul; He leads me in paths of righteousness for His name's sake.

Even though I walk through the valley of the shadow of death, I will fear no evil;

For you are with me; Your rod and your staff, they comfort me. . . .

# PART III

# The Gracious Host

*Isn't it interesting that God appears holy when he's gracious?*
—JOSEPH PRINCE

O<small>NE OF THE ENDEARING</small> and enduring aspects of the Twenty-third Psalm is the writer's use of approachable metaphors for God. God is not only pictured as the good shepherd (Part I) and the gentle guide (Part II), but also as the gracious host. We will explore and discuss this metaphor in Part III as we consider the following themes: provision (chapter 11), blessing (chapter 12), overflow (chapter 13), grace (chapter 14), and home (chapter 15). We give thanks as the gracious host invites us to a banquet held for us in the midst of our enemies, where our heads are anointed with oil and our cups are full and running over, where goodness and mercy abound, and where the hospitality of the gracious host invites us home.

Excellent hosts are described as kind, courteous, benevolent, merciful, compassionate, pleasant, and easy to be with. Such is the gracious host we encounter in verses 5 and 6 of Psalm 23—and so much more! And as we shall see, God appears holy when he is gracious, and if we have learned anything on our journey together, we know that God is indeed gracious. Let's head for the banquet and see for ourselves.

# CHAPTER 11

## *You Prepare a Table Before Me in the Presence of My Enemies—Provision*

> The gracious, eternal God permits the spirit to green and bloom and to bring forth the most marvelous fruit, surpassing anything a tongue can express and a heart conceive.
>
> —JOHANNES TAULER

### Introduction

Across the ages, Christians of all persuasions have speculated on the precise meaning of this beautiful image—a table set before us in the presence of our enemies. And would it surprise you to learn that biblical scholars have also discussed and disagreed as to the meaning? Some interpretations focus on a raging battle, imagining that a reprieve, a break in the fighting, a cease fire of sorts, has been called, giving a peaceful pause to enjoy God's provision and renewal before heading back into the fray. Others envision that we are sitting at a table surrounded by our enemies, but they are unable to do anything about it, and they are bitter about it. We take substance at God's table, all the while making faces and mocking our helpless enemies. Certainly, there have been times that I would have enjoyed this reading! Others understand this passage to suggest that it is *in* the battle that the table is set. Our enemies do not rest or stand idly by, but the banquet goes on nonetheless. Who is to say which understanding is correct; perhaps they all are, describing what we experience at one time or another.

In the meditation that follows, I am going to embrace the third interpretation—that it is in and during the battle, in the presence of our enemies, that a table is prepared for us and we are invited to come and dine. And this begs another question—what enemies are we talking about? Again, there are so many that could be mentioned, but I want us to consider the enemies of the spirit, internal enemies, and to focus on the renewal of the spirit while the battle rages. I have come to believe that we are shaped and formed in remarkable ways during our battles, gaining insights, perspectives, and experiences that could not be acquired otherwise. It is in these difficult times that we come to experience God's gracious hospitality that permits our spirits to green and bloom in ways unimagined.

## Becoming a Writer

You are reading my fifth book, something that I could not have imagined writing even six years ago. I have always loved reading, and I count some of my books among my best friends. I have always held in high esteem those who had something meaningful to say, the discipline to write a book-length manuscript, and the courage to let their friends and not-so-friends read their offerings. When you think about it, writing for publication can be an intimidating and humbling task. It surely is for me.

Honestly, while I had a fantasy from time to time that I would someday write a book, it was really a pipe dream. Being a busy academic administrator, I did my fair share of writing, but it was in the form of emails, accreditation documents, and long-range plans. A book was simply out of the question. Out of the question, that is, until I left the provost's office and joined the EdD faculty in the School of Education in the summer of 2013. To be honest, I didn't leave totally of my own accord. In effect, the boss made it clear to me that he lacked confidence in me and wanted a new provost, so I negotiated a transfer to the SOE and arrived with a bruised ego, a battered spirit, and some painful memories. Still, I pitched in, learning to teach doctoral students (I hadn't taught full time in more than twenty-five years), and to complicate matters, learning to teach online, something I had never done before. Oh, and I also needed to supervise dissertations, another new venture for me, and produce some scholarship of my own along the way. All this to say, I was overwhelmed, carrying my doubts and fearing that I would prove to be a failure again, but I set my face like flint (to paraphrase Isaiah 50:7), showed up every day, and did the best I could.

Late in that first fall semester, a good friend and colleague caught me in the hallway and casually asked, "Do you want to write a book with me?" Without even giving it a moment's thought, I responded, "Yup!" And that was it. He returned to his office and I to my teaching. Two weeks later, however, he caught me in the hallway again and said, "We have a phone call this afternoon with the editor. Can you come to my office at 2:00?" Again, I responded, "Yup!" and I showed up right on time. Thirty minutes later, a contract from the publisher was in the mail, and we had committed to submit a complete book-length manuscript in twelve weeks. Yikes!

Needless to say, I pushed aside my fears and jumped at the opportunity with gusto, writing for three hours each afternoon and an hour or so each evening. We made the deadline in good fashion, and I can't tell you how proud I was of our efforts when the authors' copies of the book arrived in the mail. I still have a picture of my friend and me holding the book, smiling like we had just won the lottery. In a way, we had. Along the way, I learned that I loved to write, and I had the organizational skills and discipline to stay with a book-length project.

With this small bit of success, I decided that I would try to write a book or two on my own, spiritual formation books sharing some of my own experiences and spiritual journey. The first book, *Morning Resolve: To Live a Simple, Sincere, and Serene Life*, almost never made it. From time to time while writing this book, I was overwhelmed with writer's doubt—feeling like I had nothing significant to say and believing that my writing was simply awful. I almost deleted the entire manuscript a time or two. Finally, I swallowed my pride and shared a chapter with two trusted friends who recognized poor writing when they saw it and were honest enough to tell me the truth about my own. They both advised me to continue, so I did. I sent book proposals off to four publishers. I received a polite rejection from one publisher and never heard back from another, but while sitting in a fast food restaurant one Tuesday six weeks later, I received emails from two publishers within five minutes of each other, each wanting to send a contract for the book. I couldn't believe it. After suffering through several years of what can only be described as miserable treatment, causing me to leave what I felt was my deep calling,

I was now going to write a spiritual formation book—and I did. My wife took a picture of me holding this book, too, and as you might guess, I was smiling like I had just won the lottery for a second time. In a way, I had. It was a banquet prepared before me in the presence of my enemies.

Fast forward to today. I am recently retired, and I am dealing with the invisibility that comes with the territory. I guess I had visions that my phone would ring off the hook and a plethora of offers and invitations would keep me busy—and in the spotlight. Not so. I find myself having to construct activities and meaning for my days. This is not a bad thing by any means, but honestly it is not what I had in mind or hoped would happen.

There is a labyrinth at a church in our town, and I walk it regularly. In medieval times, a labyrinth was a substitute for those devout souls who couldn't afford to make a pilgrimage to Jerusalem. The way a labyrinth is fashioned, there is only one way in to the center, and you must return via the same route. One spiritual practice is to carry burdens and concerns to the center, leave them there, and return with an uplifted spirit and a renewed sense of direction. Soon after I retired, I took the entirety of my professional academic career and left it in the middle of the labyrinth, feeling that it was time to move on, and returned with my own distorted hopes and dreams for retirement. Several months later, I had to retrace my steps. This time, I took my prideful hopes and dreams and left them at the center, giving them to God, trusting in the gracious host to permit my spirit to green and bloom. As I made my way out of the labyrinth, I felt the Holy Spirit speaking to me, saying, "I have given you the gifts and time to write, Patrick, and you have something helpful and hopeful to create that would not otherwise be written. Use these gifts wisely, regardless of what else you face. This is your time: this is your calling."

So, I am a writer, trusting in the gracious host who prepares a table for me *in* the presence of my enemies. As we shall see in the next section, we all nourish enemies of one kind or another, and they rarely take leave on their own. We'll examine three of the most common culprits: pride, doubts, and past failings.

## We All Have Enemies

When we think about being in the presence of our enemies, it is easy to think of a battle where we are being attacked on all sides. We can imagine the clashing of swords, chains, and armor, the sounds of reinforcements racing forward, and the cries of the wounded. We've watched many such scenes in the movies. However, I am afraid that such battle scenes distort the identities of the enemies we face each day. From time to time, it is possible to have an external enemy. Someone or something or some organization that is up to no good and intent on hurting us, breaking our spirits, and seeing us gone. Fortunately, for most of us such enemies are few and far between. I have experienced enemies like this only once or twice in my lifetime. Rather, I have come to believe that most of our enemies we face each day are internal, carried by us, nurtured by us, and the attacks come from the inside out. And since they are with us, there is nowhere we can run and hide or go to avoid them—they must be faced.

*Pride*

Perhaps the most common enemy most of us face is pride. Of course, to have feelings of satisfaction derived from our own good work or the accomplishments of our team is a good thing, but we know that pride can also result in a high and inordinate opinion of ourselves. This not only leads to a sense of superiority and importance, but also distorts our sense of reality and compels us to protect that distortion from all comers at all costs. It becomes an enemy of honest living, displayed in our conduct and bearing, and it is evidenced in the lofty way we see ourselves and our not-so-subtle insistence that others share our inflated opinion.

When such distortions occur, pride leads easily to blame. After all, if something goes wrong, it must be the fault of someone else; and if we are seen as less than perfect, it must be their faulty vision—not our own actions. Such episodes of blame construct barriers that keep us from authentic relationships, and the truth about us on the run, too. We build a fantasy world and demand that others pay the rent. There is insight and caution in Proverbs: "Pride goes before destruction, a haughty spirit before a fall" (16:18). This is sad but true, of course. The enemy we see is in us, in fact, *is* us—but we fail to make the connection because pride creates a huge blind spot, carrying the unseen and unimagined seeds of many of our own difficulties. Obviously, this enemy must be faced, and to do so takes courage, clarity, and more.

## *Doubt*

Doubt is another internal enemy many of us battle. From time to time, we doubt that others are telling us the truth. We doubt that we will ever get a fair shake. We doubt that anyone will really like us if they get to know us. We doubt that we will ever be good enough to please God. We even wonder if God really cares for us, or if there is a God at all. We all have these doubts, and certainly some of us have more than others, but doubts are part of the human experience. There is no need to panic about having doubts. They will come, you can survive them, and God can take it.

The rub comes when we let our doubts rule our lives. If we begin to believe that all our doubts are true, and we act accordingly, we invite a whole host of fears that ultimately lead to spiritual paralysis. We are frozen in place, afraid to take even the smallest steps of faith. Though we are encouraged to walk in the spirit (Gal 5:16), we just stand there, unable to summon the courage to move because the entire spiritual landscape looks like quicksand. This enemy must be faced, too.

## *Memories of Past Failings*

A third internal enemy bears mentioning—memories of past failings. Of course, none of us are perfect, so it is natural that at some time or another we will fall short of the mark, whatever the mark happens to be. That's life. I believe that memories of such events in our lives can be instructive to us, serving as both fence posts and guide posts for our spiritual journeys. In fact, we learn far more from our failings than from our successes. In this way of thinking, failings can be embraced as a source of wisdom. The key is to learn from our mistakes and then move on.

Unfortunately, the downside of failings is that rather than serving as wise teachers, we see them as indictments from an angry prosecutor, and we carry them like a scarlet letter. Instead of seeing failings as a normal part of life that offer opportunities to learn, we view them as proof that we are, indeed, a shameful failure. When we give life to memories of failings in this way, it leads to a family of regrets—why was I so stupid, I should have known better, what's the use in even trying, I'll never measure up . . . such regrets lead to apathy. The memories of past failings can be so overwhelming that we won't even try to move on. Instead, we're caught in a sad circle dance: remembering, regretting, grieving, and loathing. This enemy must be faced, too. We need to find new partners for the dance of life.

## Enemies Don't Just Go Away

We have just reviewed three of the most common enemies we face—pride, doubt, and memories of past failings. I wish I could tell you that you will wake up one morning to find that they are gone, having pulled back in full retreat or marched forward waiving the white flag of surrender. Unfortunately, that's not the way these enemies work. They must be squarely faced, and that takes wisdom and courage.

Why is it so difficult to face these internal enemies? I have come to believe that one reason is that they actually become our close companions, and we nurture them in a codependent way. Indeed, it is a one-sided relationship where we rely on these friends for emotional and self-esteem support. In a twisted sort of way, these enemies shape our sense of reality, protecting us as we try to find our way home. The problem, of course, is that they are not our friends, and they lead us down some lonely and destructive paths.

So, how do we wisely deal with these enemies? The first step is to squarely face them. Introduce yourself to them. Call them by name. Don't be afraid. Take some time to be reflective about your life. Ask the Holy Spirit to work in your life—to examine you, highlight any areas that need work, and provide the wisdom and courage to do so. As with most areas of spiritual growth, it beckons both time alone with God and time with others who understand what we face and can offer wise counsel, support, and accountability.

As we mature (a kinder way of saying, as we get older), some of the rough edges of our pride will be rubbed off. Experiences, both good and not-so-good, have a way of doing that. Still, it takes some sobering reflection and courage to admit to ourselves and to others that we have been a bit too prideful at times, and still are today more than we would like to admit. Such an honest assessment is the start of the way forward. We deal with the enemy of pride with a good dose of honesty, and then do our very best to walk humbly with God and our neighbors.

We deal with our doubts by being open about them. First, admitting that we have them, honestly sharing them with God and a safe friend or mentor. Often, we think that we're the only one in the world with certain doubts and fears, and it is both surprising and settling to hear someone we trust and admire say, "Me too." It is also helpful to take the time (often with the insight and support of others) to look back and note that most of our doubts and fears didn't materialize in any meaningful way or they were simply inconsequential for our spiritual journey.

We move forward when we are honest about pride and open about doubts and fears, so what about the memories of our failings and the shame that so often accompanies them? The antidote is kindness—kindness that we extend to ourselves. I think it is one of the hardest things we must learn to do. It often requires the wisdom and support of others, but to be as kind with ourselves and to ourselves as we are with others is the rich soil where confidence, courage, and self-esteem can take root and bloom. We all have failings, but we are not failures.

Our enemies won't simply go away, but they can be faced and countered with a good portion of honesty, openness, and kindness. It is a spiritual process, so it won't happen all at once, but we can deal effectively with them. They do not have to be our lifelong companions.

## Our Table Is Waiting

We have all heard that someone is their own worst enemy. To the extent that we carry and feed such enemies as pride, doubt, and failings, this saying holds true for most of us at one time or another. The bad news is that they won't just go away on their own; the good news is that if we deal with them forthrightly with honestly, openness, and kindness, we don't have to battle them constantly on our spiritual journeys. Time, they say, heals all wounds. In this case, time and intention are great healers.

And there's more good news. A table is set for us *in the presence* of our enemies. The invitation is not for us to come once we have eliminated all our enemies, but in the midst of them, so bring them to the table. The important thing is to come! The banquet is not reserved for the perfect. This is good news, indeed. The gracious host bids us to come to the table enemies and all, and if we do, we will find a veritable banquet set before us. All we have to do is show up. God's gracious hospitality will allow our spirits to green and bloom and bring forth marvelous fruit in the most unlikely times and in the most difficult places. Thanks be to God!

## Scripture

In what follows, three very different stories from Scripture will be offered as a way for us to contemplate about the enemies we carry and nurture: pride, doubt, and past failings. As we will see, honesty, openness, and kindness can be effective antidotes. And remember, an antidote is something that can counteract a form of poisoning, especially when it is our own spirit, our sense of reality, and our relationship with God that is suffering.

## King Saul—Pride

Soon after David, the shepherd boy, killed the mighty warrior, Goliath, with a sling and five smooth stones, all the towns of Israel along the return route to Jerusalem celebrated the miraculous victory. After all, by that time everyone had heard of Goliath and knew what would happen to their town and to their families if the Philistines prevailed. The women poured out into the streets and met the army with joyful songs, singing and dancing with tambourines and lutes. They sang, "Saul has slain his thousands, and David his tens of thousands" (1 Sam 18:7). What happened next was truly sad, but predictable: "Saul was very angry: this refrain galled him. 'They have credited David with tens of thousands,' he thought, 'but me with only thousands. What more can he get but the kingdom?' And from that time on Saul kept a jealous eye on David" (1 Sam 18:8–9). This refrain galled Saul and he kept a jealous eye on David. Why? Surely Saul knew that David loved him and his family, especially his son, Jonathan, and David was as loyal and trustworthy as anyone could possibly be. Why then was Saul so jealous? I think it started when the Israelites celebrated David's bravery and victory. That galled Saul. It wounded his pride and his own sense that he had to be acknowledged as the best at everything, and this led straight away to jealousy. Pride, we have been told, comes before a fall—and fall he did.

I have often wondered if things would have been different for Israel if King Saul had swallowed his pride and joined in the celebration, appreciating David for his courage, resourcefulness, and loyalty. Being honest about one's pride is not easy, but the consequences for not doing so are legend.

### The Desperate Father—Doubt

In one of the most remarkable stories in the New Testament, Mark relates Jesus' encounter with a desperate father whose son was possessed by an evil spirit (Mark 9:14–29). The disciples tried to exorcise the spirit, but they could not. Jesus saw the commotion and asked what was going on. When he was told about the disciples' failure to heal the boy, the father asked Jesus for help—*if he could*. Jesus responded that all things are possible to those who believe. To this, the father responded with as much honesty as I have ever encountered, "I do believe; help me overcome my unbelief!" (Mark 9:24).

Certainly, this was a courageous act of faith and a display of doubt at the same time. After all, he did want Jesus to heal his tormented son, so it took a great deal of courage to express his sincere doubts that anything could be done. Jesus chided him a bit by asking, "If I can?" and then proceeded to heal his son (9:23). There's a lesson here for all of us. Jesus wasn't put off by the father's doubts or his openness about them. He was honest, and Jesus honestly responded. In many ways, faith and doubt are two sides of the same coin. In my way of thinking, having faith implies some dimension of doubt, too. Otherwise it would be called certainty, not faith. And I have come to believe that God is a good, kind, and gracious host—even with our doubts, perhaps especially with our doubts. He sets a table before us in the presence of our enemies, and bids us to bring our doubts and come. Lord, we do believe; help us overcome our unbelief.

### Peter—Memories of Past Failings

Near the end of the Gospel of John, we find Jesus early in the morning on the shore of the Sea of Galilee, waiting by a warm fire for some of the disciples to return from fishing (21:1–14). After cooking some breakfast for the hungry fishermen, he had a very intimate conversation with Peter, the one who had denied knowing him three times during the night when he was arrested and sentenced to death (21:15–25). Surely, this multiple betrayal must have haunted Peter; it would any of us. But Jesus didn't mention Peter's failings—not even once. Instead, Jesus asked Peter three times if he loved him. Of course, Peter said that he did, and Jesus told Peter to "feed my lambs" (21:15), "take care of my sheep" (21:16), and "feed my sheep" (21:17). Instead of reminding Peter of his failings, he pointed to his calling, to be the shepherd of the flock. He had work to do. No time for regret; others needed him.

I deeply believe that God is more interested in what we are called to do than in our past failings. That's good news for all of us, isn't it? God is the gracious host who beckons us to come for breakfast and stay for lunch. We will be fed in the presence of our enemies, even if the list of our failings is long and mostly of our own doing. Even so, there are no failures at the table of the gracious host.

## Some Practical Advice

Before we conclude this meditation on the provision of grace in the presence of our enemies, I want to share just a few words of practical advice. Nothing that follows is particularly earthshaking, but I trust these words will be helpful to all of us as we make our way to the table, bringing our enemies with us as we do our best to confront them.

### Name Your Enemies

I have come to believe that the way forward starts with some honest reflection and meditation—setting aside some daily quiet time, intentionally listening to God and reflecting honestly and humbly about our lives. Make it a daily practice. Listening is difficult for most of us. We are much better at talking, especially to God, but the rich soil for spiritual growth is in the listening, while we make an honest assessment of our lives. When we are still and take stock of our journey, I truly believe that the Holy Spirit will speak. Things will come to mind, things that need to be faced. Face them squarely. Name them for what they are. They need to be called out before they can be culled out. Ask God for direction and strength to deal with them honestly and openly. It is in these hours of sober reflection and supplication that insight and courage come.

### Share Your Doubts

We all have doubts, so don't be ashamed to acknowledge them—and to share them, too. We often carry our doubts like a dark secret, thinking that we are the only one in the world who have them. When we share our doubts, however, it keeps our own faith alive and active, and we find that they are not life-threatening. In fact, they energize our daily walk, and they are good for others to hear. After all, they have their own doubts, too.

When we exercise the courage to share our doubts and fears, others will often say, "me too!," ushering in deeper conversations and forming stronger bonds of friendships and support. Such formative conversations depend on honesty and openness, and I have come to believe that they are an important spiritual practice. Surely, we need to spend time alone with God, but we also need to spend time in serious conversations with our friends and neighbors about spiritual things that matter, including our doubts and questions. Just as the gracious host sets a table before us in the presence of our enemies, we can invite those who journey with us to our table, too. Good conversations around the kitchen table with soup and bread can renew the soul.

## Deal With Your Blind Spots

Most of the new cars sold today have blind spot indicators in the side view mirrors. When something is in your blind spot, a little light appears as if to say, "Watch out, you can't see the danger that is nearby." I think we can all agree that it would be nice to have our own spiritual blind spot indicators, too. After all, it is almost impossible to deal with your own blind spots precisely because we are blind to them—thus the name.

The good news is that it is possible to develop blind spot indicators. Sometimes, God will directly speak to you and point out areas in your life in need of correction, but more often than not, God works indirectly—through our friends, mentors, and spiritual directors, and through reading, preaching, and even music. Others do see how we live and can point out inconsistencies and provide accountability if given the permission to do so. Having someone in your life who knows you well enough to point out your blind spots and walk with you as you address them is truly a gracious gift. As it turns out, spiritual formation is always a communal act.

## Apologize Forward

Let me offer one additional word of practical advice: if you can't go back and make things right, apologize forward. By this I mean that sometimes we have memories of past failings and carry regrets about treating others shabbily or crossing the line in a place or two, yet there is too much water under the bridge to go back and make things right. It is simply impossible or pointless to do so.

How then can we deal with these regrets? I would suggest a three-step approach. First, be candid with God about your regrets. Name them specifically and make time to sit with them before God, letting the Holy Spirit speak to you and affirm that there is nothing you can do to make the gracious host stop loving you. You are invited to the table in the presence of your enemies. Your regrets are no secret of God, and despite your own misgivings, you are the honored guest, even when you feel like an imposter.

Second, think carefully about how you might go back and at least express regret to someone who has been hurt by your actions. This is tough business, I know, but sometimes this is the most healing and formative act you can undertake. Often, your apology will come as a surprise to them because it is a much bigger event in own your life than in theirs. That's OK, too. It is never too late to apologize and receive forgiveness; it will clear the slate and offer you a fresh start.

Finally, forgive yourself and move on. For most of us, this is the hardest thing of all to do. We can extend an olive branch to others, but we can't or won't forgive ourselves and accept grace from others. One of the most formative spiritual practices I know is to humbly ask for forgiveness and accept it when it is offered. And the best response to grace that is offered to us is to simply move on—with wisdom, humility, and a deeper appreciation for the gifts of the gracious host.

So, what do we do when we can't go back and make things right? This is often the case. My advice is to apologize forward. That is, think carefully and prayerfully about how you might extend grace to someone else, someone nearby. If you can't go back, reach out and join the "me too" cloud of witnesses. After all, that is all of us.

## Conclusion

We are so thankful that a table has been set before us in the presence of our enemies, and we acknowledge that most of our enemies are internal and of our own doing. We looked at three internal enemies that are often nurtured: pride, doubt, and memories of past failings, and noted that they won't go away on their own but can be addressed with honesty, openness, and kindness. And we celebrated that we are not required to be perfect (enemy-free) in order to come to the table. The invitation stands—just as we are.

We then noted three stories from Scripture that illustrate the enemies we often carry: King Saul—pride, The Desperate Father—doubt, and Peter—memories of past failings. And we offered several words of practical advice: name your enemies, share your doubts, deal with your blind spots, and apologize forward if you can't go back. At the end of the day, the gracious host prepares a table for us in the presence of our enemies. All we have to do is respond to the invitation. It is a "come as you are" celebration of grace upon grace, and we are the honored guest.

## Questions for Reflection and Discussion:

1. Which of the three enemies discussed in this chapter are you most likely to carry with you: pride, doubt, or past failings?
2. Why is it that we carry and nurture such unhelpful enemies?
3. Do you have a regular time and place for daily introspection—a time you set aside to hear from the Holy Spirit? How might such a time be constructed in your schedule, busy as it is?
4. Who would be a trusted friend, mentor, or spiritual director that you could safely talk to about dealing with your enemies? Where might such a person be found?
5. Why do you think it is so much easier to forgive others than to accept grace and forgiveness ourselves? Could it have something to do with our own pride, doubt, or memories of past failings?

## Psalm 23

The LORD is my shepherd; I shall not want.

He makes me lie down in green pastures; He leads me beside still waters.

He restores my soul; He leads me in paths of righteousness for His name's sake.

Even though I walk through the valley of the shadow of death, I will fear no evil;

For you are with me; Your rod and your staff, they comfort me.

You prepare a table before me in the presence of my enemies . . .

## CHAPTER 12

## *You Anoint My Head With Oil—Blessing*

To give someone a blessing is the most significant affirmation we can offer.
—HENRI NOUWEN

### Introduction

To have your head anointed with oil affirms that you are not just a guest on the list with a reservation at a side table, but *the* honored guest. It is personal—it is to be blessed. In this chapter we will explore the meaning of this metaphor and consider why giving someone a blessing is the most significant affirmation we can offer, and why at times it is so difficult to receive a blessing and even harder to extend one to someone else. As it turns out, it is a deeply formative spiritual practice, and practice does make perfect.

### Family Blessings

It was Memorial Day. My mother went out to the driveway to raise the flag. She did so on several occasions throughout the year—Martin Luther King Jr. Day, George Washington's Birthday, Memorial Day, Independence Day, Veterans Day, certain local events, and sometimes just to see Old Glory fly. She loved celebrations, and she loved flying the flag.

The tall flagpole in our front yard served two purposes. It displayed the flag, of course, and it housed a large flood light that allowed us to play basketball in the driveway late into the night. My uncle and his family lived next door. We must have kept them up way past their usual bedtime from time to time, but they never complained—at least not to us. It seems that everyone in our neighborhood admired the huge flagpole in our front yard, or at least we thought they did.

One time as my mother stepped back to admire the flag, she tripped and fell on the driveway, breaking her hip. She was rushed to the hospital, where complications ensued. She ended up in a coma on life support, ushering in a bittersweet ordeal for the family. My father had to decide if and when to take my mother, his partner for over fifty years, off life support. After consulting with the doctors, he called a family meeting. As we gathered together, my wife offered to step outside since she wasn't actually a part of the family. (We had been married for only a few years and lived in California, away from any family members.) My father looked directly at her and said, "No, you need to stay. You *are* family!" She was and she did.

We all agreed that Mom would not want to be kept alive by some machine, so the decision was made. The doctor told us that she would likely only live for an hour or two, maybe less, so we prepared ourselves for that eventuality. However, she remained in a coma for almost two weeks. We took turns keeping vigil, and by the end, all of us were physically and emotionally exhausted. A nurse told us that it was unclear if Mom could hear anything or not, so it might be good to sing a few of her favorite songs. We borrowed a guitar and a hymnal from a local pastor, and my wife and I sang some of her favorite hymns—"Great Is Thy Faithfulness," "Glory to His Name," "Blessed Assurance," and "Victory in Jesus." To this day, I don't know if the nurse suggested that we sing for my mother's sake or for our own, but the singing did comfort and nourish our weary spirits in ways that are difficult to describe or explain. I hope it did the same for my mother, too.

Near the end of the second week, my wife and I decided to take a long drive. We needed some distance from the daily hospital routine. We drove over to Lake Michigan and spent some time by the water. As we were returning, we decided to make a quick stop at the hospital, even though it was late in the day. We were there for less than five minutes when a nurse rushed in and told us that my mother was failing and would be gone in just a matter of minutes. The nurse said that someone should say something to Mom, letting her know that it was OK to let go. The others in the room looked at me, so I stepped forward, took my mother's hand, and said: "It's OK, Mom. It's time to go. We'll take care of Pop, and we'll be OK, too. You can go now, there's no need to fight anymore. We love you very much." It was the best blessing I could come up with. Honestly, I do not know if she heard me or not, but in less than twenty seconds, she was gone.

Two and a half years later, I received a call from my younger brother: "If you want to talk to Dad while he's alive, you'd better come right away. He hasn't much time left." When I first walked into his room, my father didn't recognize me. I was met with a blank stare, and he quickly closed his eyes and went back to sleep. I told the others that they could go and get something to eat. I would be happy to sit by his bed and look after him in the event he awoke. In about an hour, he opened his eyes and said, "Well, hello, Patrick. It is so good to see you!" His mind was sharp, and he was totally present. It was a blessing. We had a wonderful, far-ranging conversation. When I told him that I had an interview with a university in Oregon, he raised up in bed and said, "Oh, I'll go with you. We can leave tonight!" He always loved a road trip.

I asked him if he knew that he didn't have much time left. He said that he did. I asked him if he had his affairs in order. He said that he did. I then asked if there was anyone that he would like to speak to while he could. He thought for a moment and then said: "No, I don't want to talk to anyone, but could you bring Smokey [my brother's dog] over. I miss that dog." Actually, that wasn't too surprising. He always loved dogs, and Smokey and Dad had become constant companions in the last year. Animals were not allowed in the facility, but my brother brought Smokey to the window. The visit really lifted Dad's spirits.

The next morning, my wife and I stopped by to say goodbye to Dad before we left for home. After talking for a few minutes, he took my wife's hand and said, "Thank you for taking good care of my son. Now I won't have to worry about him anymore." He paused, catching his breath, looked Lori right in the eyes, and continued, "And remember, you *are* part of this family." These were the last words he ever spoke to us, and they were, and are to this day, a blessing.

\* \* \*

Blessings come to us in all shapes and sizes, and at unexpected times, too. We often associate blessings with deathbed experiences, and that they are. As death approaches, small talk becomes irrelevant and fades away, creating space for serious and sometimes difficult conversations, but they are formative for good or for ill, and never forgotten. In this chapter, we will first examine the metaphor of the gracious host who anoints our heads with oil, and then suggest that giving and receiving a blessing need not be limited to the deathbed. In fact, it is a life-giving spiritual practice, a sacred act of affirmation.

## The Gracious Host

When the host anoints your head with oil, you can be sure that the banquet is in your honor. You are, in fact, the honored guest, even in the midst of your enemies. It is the most significant affirmation a host can offer to anyone. It is, indeed, a public blessing.

Of course, anointing someone's head with oil had several significant spiritual meanings in Old Testament times. It could mean that someone was God's choice for a particular leadership position. For example, Samuel anointed Saul (1 Sam 9–10) and later David as King of Israel (1 Sam 16:1–13). Ancient prophets were also anointed with oil, signifying that they were called, set apart, and consecrated, making them a spiritual leader and their work a sacred obligation. Think of Nathan who was sent by God to confront King David about his relationship with Bathsheba and the much-too-convenient death of her husband (2 Sam 12). Of course, calling a king to accountability was risky business in those days (and in these days, too), but prophets were purveyors of the truth regardless of the consequences. Without their courage, something very sacred would have been lost.

But throwing a celebration in someone's honor was different still. It wasn't a divine obligation. Rather, it was a choice made by the host, and it signaled that the honored guest was considered to be special and worthy of the honor. It was an intentional, particular blessing, and it still is.

When we speak of blessings today, we often mean encouragement—"she has been a blessing to me." And it can mean approval or support for something, as in asking someone's blessing to undertake a new ministry assignment, to pursue a new job, or to marry. Good and loyal friends have been recognized as a blessing since ancient times. And sometimes even our most difficult trials may later prove to be a blessing in disguise. Indeed, blessings come in ways known and unknown, but they are gifts of God's grace shared among us as we make our way home. I have come to believe that choosing to offer someone a blessing is one of the most formative and affirming spiritual practices we can undertake, and learning to accept a blessing gracefully even more formative still.

## Blessings

Indeed, we recognize that offering a blessing is a highly formative spiritual discipline. Why, then, is it so rarely practiced today, and why is receiving a blessing so uncomfortable and even a bit embarrassing? I think the answer in large part is that receiving a blessing is deeply affirming but intensely personal. When someone looks you squarely in the eyes, touches your hand or puts their hand on your shoulder, it communicates that something very important and personal is being shared—that you are loved, that you are needed, that you have gifts, that you are part of the family, that you have a new name. There is no way to argue or rationalize it away. You receive it full on and your spirit soaks it up, even if you feel a twinge of embarrassment at the time. You'll recover.

In a day when most of our communication is with the aid of a screen of one kind or another, what I call i-communication, blessings are given eyeball to eyeball, with what I call eye-communication. This type of communication makes us uncomfortable because it is unusually singular and personal. Thus, receiving and giving blessings takes practice and spiritual courage, too. After all, no one wants to come across as a kook.

My younger brother and I had the privilege of playing college basketball together. Sometimes after a game, someone would come up and congratulate us on a good game. I would always play it off, pointing out that many mistakes were made and we needed to get better. My brother turned to me on one occasion and told me that I was not being gracious. He said that I should simply say, "Thank you very much. I appreciate it. That means a lot to me." It was sage advice, and I would say that it holds true as the best way to receive a blessing, too—"Thank you very much. I appreciate it. That means a lot to me." That's really all you need to say. Sometimes that is all you can say. Of course, blessings will stay with you and work on you, and they should. It usually takes a while to let an honest blessing sink in. Sometimes it takes a day or two, sometimes a month or so, and sometimes years. Luckily for all of us, blessings have staying power.

Jesus taught that it is more blessed to give than to receive (Acts 20:35), and for most of us, it is more difficult to give a blessing than to receive one. Why? Part of the answer is that we have very little experience with blessings of any kind, so we are out of our comfort zone. It is a learned practice. My wife is a giver of blessings. On many occasions, we would be standing near our front door after an evening of fellowship with someone we loved, and my wife would turn to them and offer a blessing. At first, it caught me off-guard and I must admit that I was a bit embarrassed just standing there as a witness, but I saw the impact of the blessings and resolved to be giver of blessings myself. It did take some practice, but I found that my intent to bless someone was always accepted with grace and appreciation, even when what I said came out awkwardly. Authenticity has a way of carrying the day.

I'll later offer some practical advice for offering a blessing, so suffice it here to say the offering a blessing is one of the most personal and powerful spiritual disciplines that we can undertake. It shapes and forms others in significant ways, and it will shape us, too. And as with most things that we practice, we get better at it when we do.

## Scripture

There is a website that lists seventy-three Bible verses about blessings. Another website lists thirty-four top Bible verses about blessings, and yet another promotes the top twenty. They do not disclose what criteria were used to cull the list from seventy-three to thirty-four or to twenty, or what constitutes a "top blessing," but we can say with certainty that blessings play a prominent role in our faith tradition, and always have.

And, of course, there are many kinds of blessings—dedications, affirmations, requests for protection, approvals, and even a look into the future, like giving someone a new name. In what follows, we'll look at three occasions where persons were given a new name as a blessing and in anticipation of their future, and as we will see, it was not always because the person lived a blameless life of faith. In that, we can all take heart as we make our way home as best we can.

## Abram and Sari

If we know anything about Abraham, we know that he was a man of faith. In one of the most profound and honest tributes extended to anyone in the Bible, we find this in Hebrews 11:8: "By faith Abraham, when called to go to a place he would later receive as an inheritance, obeyed and went even though he did not know where he was going." This verse speaks to so many of us because we've been there, too, or are there still.

Abraham was faithful and obedient to God's call, but his name wasn't always Abraham—it was Abram until he was ninety-nine years old. The Lord appeared to him and told him that he was no longer to be called Abram (High Father). From that day forward, he would be called Abraham (Father of a Multitude), which came as a great surprise to him given his age and the fact that he and his wife, Sari, had no children. And Sari (My Precious) would have a new name, too, Sarah (Mother of Nations). This was a prediction and a promise—a blessing (Gen 17–18).

In many ways, the entire event must have seemed and felt a bit pretentious, but there it was—new names, a prediction of the future, a promise from God, a blessing. And within the year, much to the surprise and delight of Abraham and Sarah, the blessing became a reality with the birth of their son, Isaac, who is listed in the genealogy of Jesus found in the Gospel of Matthew. God gave new names, offered a blessing, and the rest is history.

## Jacob

Jacob was Abraham's grandson, but he didn't follow closely in the family tradition of faithfulness. It seems that he lived up to the meaning of his name—supplanter, conniver, or simply "he cheats," and cheat he did (Gen 25–33). You may recall that he talked his exhausted and famished brother, Esau, into trading his birthright for a bowl of soup, and tricked his father, Isaac, into giving him the family blessings, although it belonged to his elder brother. He undertook some shady business dealings with and against his father-in-law, Laban, and on occasion even resorted to a bit of magic in an effort to help his flocks produce more offspring. And when he finally decided to return to his family home, fleeing Laban's wrath, to whom he fled to escape his brother's wrath in the first place, he sent his family and livestock on ahead to meet Esau, who had sworn to kill him on sight. Using your family as a human shield is not the most honorable or courageous way to return home.

That night, alone, Jacob entered into a titanic wrestling match with someone he didn't know. They wrestled all night. Near daybreak, the man asked Jacob to let him go, to which Jacob countered, "I will not let you go until you bless me" (Gen 32:26b), realizing by this time that this was more than just a human contest. The man asked Jacob for his name. Knowing what his name meant, this could not have been an easy thing for Jacob to reveal, but he admitted who he was (the conniver). In return he received a blessing and a new name: "Your name will no longer be Jacob, but Israel, because you have struggled with God and with men and have overcome" (32:28).

I think we identify with the story of Jacob because this is our story, too. Jacob crossed the line and fell short so many times that it was difficult for him to know where the lines were drawn or if there were any lines at all. At the end of the day, in the middle of the night, all he could do was hold on, reveal his true identity, and ask for a blessing. All we can do is to say, "me too," and trust in the gracious host who anoints our heads with oil, who looks us squarely in the eyes, knows our names and our stories, and gives us new names anyway. It is a blessing. It is what God does.

## Simon Peter

I think some of us are like Abraham, faithful saints come hell or high water. Some of us are more like Jacob, falling short time after time, but holding on as best we can. Many of us are somewhere in between. So was one of Jesus' closest disciples, Simon, son of Jonah. After he confessed that Jesus was the Christ (Matt 16:16), Jesus blessed him and gave him a new name, Peter. He was to be the rock upon which Jesus would build his church (16:18), and he was, and Jesus did.

But Peter also came up short on more than one occasion, and sometimes in very public ways and unfortunate moments. Perhaps that's why even though he had a new name, Jesus called him Simon every once in a while. For example, in Matthew 17:25 we find, "When Peter came into the house, Jesus was the first to speak. "What do you think, Simon?" he asked" (17:25). Why did Jesus refer to him as both Simon and Peter? To be honest, no one knows exactly why, but here's my sense of it. Sometimes Peter was the rock, and other times he was more of a rolling stone, unpredictable to say the least. He was both Simon and Peter. Peter was full of faith and good intentions, but sometimes, at the most critical moments, Simon would appear. It wasn't a lack of belief. It wasn't a lack of commitment to Jesus and his ministry. He just came up short every once in a while.

Let's be honest. That's our story, too. We are believers but as unpredictable as Simon Peter. It's good to remember that he was given a new name and an important calling anyway—to be the rock upon which the church would be built.

I'm convinced that the gracious host knows that we're not perfect, yet our heads are anointed with oil and we are given a new name, not because of who we are or what we have done, but for what the future holds in store for us. It is a promise and a blessing. We each have a calling. Thanks be to God.

## Words of Practical Advice

Before we conclude this chapter on blessings, let me offer just a few pointers as you think about the power and practice of giving and receiving blessings.

### Be Intentional

Think carefully about the context of offering a blessing to someone. Are they about to embark on an important trip or a life adventure, or are they about to face a difficult or painful situation? Will they be in a situation where spiritual questions will be asked or offered? Think about the surroundings and context for offering a blessing and be sure that you are in a space and at a time when your blessing will be heard and appreciated. If you are at home, a good time is often just as your guests are standing by the front door and about to go to their car, a time when you would naturally say goodbye and extend well-wishes. Be intentional or the moment can slip by quickly.

### Be Prepared

I am aware that some feel that offering a blessing should be guided by the Holy Spirit, and as such it must be spontaneous. I must disagree. While I do believe that there are times when we are prompted to say something on the spot or called on at the last moment, I also believe that there is great value in preparation, organization, even practice. I can't think of a single reason why the Holy Spirit would be against careful thought, advance planning, and a rehearsal or two in front of the mirror. Most of us are not spontaneously eloquent. Why should we avoid choosing our words carefully and offering them articulately, especially if we can anticipate the opportunity to speak into someone's life? Be intentional and be prepared.

## Be Courageous

I can attest that there have been times when I was intentional and prepared to offer a blessing, but as the anticipated moment arrived, I stood by silently rather than leaning in and speaking what was on my heart and mind. Why? I was afraid that I would embarrass someone, particularly myself. I saw the opportunity and conveniently let it slide by. In every such case, it led to regret—my regret. The only advice I can offer is to affirm that when the moment arrives, your palms might be sweaty, and your heart might beat a bit faster. Remember, that's normal. Swallow hard, step up, and say what's on your mind anyway. Don't let your nerves nullify the moment. Be intentional, be prepared, and be courageous.

## Be Gracious

If you are in the position of receiving a blessing from someone, be gracious. Look the giver in the eyes and simply say "Thank you." There is no need to say anything else. No need to tell your host that they really don't know you or understand your situation. Simply accept the blessing for what it is, even if it is misguided. Carry the blessing with you and appreciate the intent of the giver. Always be gracious, regardless of the circumstances.

## Be Discerning

Finally, it is important to be mindful of who you permit to speak into your life and what their motives may be. To be forthright, not all "words from the Lord" are from the Lord. I hope you understand. There are times when the extension of a word or blessing is more about the giver than the receiver. In such cases, it is important to think carefully about what has been offered and consider the source, and it is often helpful to seek counsel from a mentor or spiritual director. Be gracious but discern carefully.

## Conclusion

It is the gracious host who sets a table before us in the presence of our enemies and then anoints our heads with oil, announcing to everyone that we are the honored guests. It is certainly a divine act of spiritual care. And when we extend a blessing, it is the most significant affirmation that we can offer anyone. It is a spiritual practice with an immediate impact and a long memory, and it shapes and forms the giver in powerful and personal ways.

However, it is often a bit awkward to offer someone a blessing, taking us outside of our comfort zone, and it isn't a discipline that is modeled widely, especially in an age of i-communication. I have found that the most effective blessings are built on relationships, up close and personal, eyeball to eyeball. They are conveyed with eye-communication. And receiving a blessing from someone can be a bit embarrassing, too. As it turns out, both giving and receiving a blessing are learned spiritual disciplines, and we get better at them the more we engage in the practice.

At the end of the day, we can affirm that as we offer and accept blessings, the kingdom comes to us in ways unimagined. We were challenged long ago to love God with everything we have, and our neighbor as ourselves (Deut 6:5; Matt 22:37–40). I can think of no better way to love our neighbors than to anoint their heads with oil, to offer them a blessing, and allow them to bless us, too.

## Questions for Reflection and Discussion:

1. Why do you think blessings have such spiritual power?
2. What is the most powerful blessing you have personally witnessed? Why was it so powerful?
3. Has anyone ever given you a new name—literally or figuratively? What is it?
4. Would you rather give or receive a blessing? Why so?

5. Sometimes we see more in others than they see in themselves. How might you turn your insight into a blessing for someone this week?

## Psalm 23

The Lord is my shepherd; I shall not want.

He makes me lie down in green pastures; He leads me beside still waters.

He restores my soul; He leads me in paths of righteousness for His name's sake.

Even though I walk through the valley of the shadow of death, I will fear no evil;

For you are with me; Your rod and your staff, they comfort me.

You prepare a table before me in the presence of my enemies;

You anoint my head with oil . . .

## CHAPTER 13

## *My Cup Runs Over—Overflow*

No life of faith can be lived privately.
There must be overflow into the lives of others.

—EUGENE PETERSON

### Introduction

As the host prepares to offer a toast, the first glass to be filled belongs to the guest of honor, and the glass is not just filled, but filled to overflowing, signifying "there's a lot more where this comes from." It is an image worth keeping in mind as we explore together the overwhelming overflow of God's grace and consider the amazing fact that we, all of us, are and will be the guests of honor at the Lord's table. Certainly, "there's a lot more where this comes from," as anyone who has been blessed by the gracious host can attest. From the fullness of his grace we have all received one blessing after another—grace upon grace—as John puts it (1:16).

In this chapter, we will share a story about a gracious person who was dearly loved, and upon retirement received one unexpected blessing after another. In many ways, it is a picture of God's grace at work in our lives, too, a picture of the kingdom. Then we'll examine the meaning of the word *overflow* and highlight the connection between the overflow of God's love and grace that is extended to each of us, and how we might model that overflow in worship, in spiritual growth, and in service to others. As we will see, this divine connection between the overflow of God's grace that is extended to us and the overflow of grace that we offer to others make each relationship, each interaction, each activity, sacred. May we all live in such a graceful way that it is obvious to those we meet—"There's a lot more where this comes from," knowing full well that the source of the overflow in our lives is God's abundant grace. Indeed, once this is recognized, no life of faith can be lived privately.

## A Retirement Celebration

Snapper was the most dearly loved university administrator I have ever known. I was in my mid-thirties and he was nearing retirement when we met, but we immediately hit it off. He soon became not only my mentor and role model, but one of my closest friends. He was the most kind, encouraging, and humble person I have ever met, and whenever I was with him, it seemed like I was the only person in the world and it made his day to be able to spend a few minutes with me. His calendar was terribly full, but he was never too busy for a chat. And it was the same with every person he met. He was everybody's good friend.

We called him Snapper because he carried a small leather coin pouch in the front pocket of his suit pants and would snap and unsnap the pouch during casual conversations. At one point, I even looked into purchasing one for myself, but it didn't seem to work for me. I guess I just wasn't the snapper type.

In the year leading up to his retirement, he shared with me that while he would be OK in retirement, things would be very tight. Salaries were terribly low at the struggling university where we served, and the retirement program, such as it was, didn't provide much financial security. I knew there would be no room for luxuries like a new set of books or travel, and as soon as he retired, even though he truly loved the university community, he and his wife planned to move to a small rural community about 600 miles away, where they could afford to buy a small house. I knew immediately that we needed to give him the best retirement celebration we could muster, and we set out to provide him a few extravagances before he left.

At the celebration, a faculty member dressed up in a lime green leisure suit, another Snapper fashion statement. It was all in good fun, and he joined in the merriment. The skits were followed with heartfelt tributes from faculty, staff, and administrators. We all agreed that he would be sorely missed. He simply made our life together better. Then, on behalf of the faculty, Snapper was presented with a set of the Great Books and a set of the Harvard Classics. These two sets were presented one book at a time, and he broke into tears as he saw his colleagues coming to the head table from all over the room, carrying a book for him and extending good wishes to him. It was truly a moment. And the president announced that an anonymous donor had donated enough frequent flyer miles for Snapper and Mrs. Snapper to fly to England, and the university had arranged for a host to accompany them and would cover their lodging in London and Oxford. Snapper was speechless. It was an overflow of generosity from those who had been graced by his kind spirit.

What happened next simply took the cake. Several members from the physical plant crew came forward. These men were dedicated, blue-collar tradesmen who worked hard all year long, even though they were sadly underpaid. Everyone in Plant Services loved Snapper because he saw them—he always talked to them and treated them with dignity and respect. They announced that the two beautiful book sets each deserved a custom-made book shelf, something they intended to build themselves, and when the bookshelves were finished, several had volunteered to take their vacations in order to deliver the shelves to his new home 600 miles away.

And they told Snapper that they would be coming in two trucks, so there was enough room to bring along the necessary supplies to build a deck and a gazebo for his new home, and they intended to construct it while they were there if Mrs. Snapper would bake one of her famous apple pies. She said that she would. Now we were all in tears.

And finally, they joked about how often Snapper would visit Plant Services and make some comment about the red Ford pickup driven by the physical plant director. It wasn't new, but it was beautiful. Snapper loved to be chauffeured around campus in the red truck, ostensibly to inspect the grounds, but everyone knew that he just loved to ride in that truck. They told Snapper that they had discovered a good deal on a truck of the same make and model, and, with the help of some of their suppliers, came up with enough money to purchase the truck. It was being restored and repainted that very week. They would use it to bring some of the supplies to his house and then leave it with Snapper for safe keeping. After all, it seemed like every self-respecting retiree in that small town drove a pickup, and they wanted Snapper to blend in with the local folk. They also suggested that he should leave his lime green leisure suit behind and look into getting a pair of bib overalls. He smiled and said that he would.

Truly, it was blessing upon blessing. The following summer, I had the privilege of sitting on Snapper's deck and being chauffeured around town in his red pickup. Snapper said over and over that he just couldn't believe the overflow of generosity he received, and every time he drove to town, he thought of that retirement celebration. I smiled and told him that it was simply a small demonstration of the overflow of kindness and grace that he had shown all of us. Sometimes the flow goes both ways. Snapper just smiled as he opened and shut his coin purse, now in the front pocket of his grey-striped overalls. Truly, his cup was full and running over, and so was mine.

## The Overflow of God's Spirit

There are many ways to think about God's care for us and work in us—as guide, shepherd, teacher, healer, comforter, friend, and counselor, to name just a few. It is less often that we think of God's work in terms of a flow, or to be more precise, an overflow, yet there is much here to help us understand how God's spirit works in us and how we are to respond to the blessings upon blessings that come our way. As it turns out, the key is to let God's spirit flow through us and overflow into the lives of others, as Peterson suggests in this chapter's epigraph. It is how the flow remains fresh and life-giving.

Air and water are life-giving entities. We can't live without them, and their flow is critical. Without it, air and water can become stale and stagnate. So it is with the spirit of God that flows in us and through us, and into the lives of others. Of course, it is not that God's spirit becomes stagnant or stale when the flow is impeded; it is our spirits that suffer. Therefore, it is important to be mindful of the spiritual overflow in our lives, and to embrace it full-faced, breathing deeply and taking in the spiritual nourishment it offers.

Of course, overflow has several meanings—some good, some not so good. For example, when overflow refers to flooding or damage or tragedy, too much is not a good thing. However, when we think about overflow as abundant, unexpected, unthinkable, and unbelievable, we can embrace all the overflow that comes our way. God's Spirit works in us, powered and sustained by an ocean of grace. Yet we often come to this ocean with a small basin, not recognizing or taking full advantage of all that God is offering to us.

In chapter 2, we examined some of these flowing possibilities that we can embrace. We began with an assessment of our own gifts and abilities that we have been given, our intuition, and the still small voice that speaks to us, guides us, and corrects us. There is the wisdom that comes from our own experiences, the experiences of others, and from Scripture. There are the passions, dreams, and desires that energize the opportunities that come our way, and our relationships that offer guidance, instruction, comfort, correction, fellowship, and service. And we noted that our own local faith community can be a major source of spiritual flow since it is a reservoir for so many of the possibilities just mentioned. As we engage our faith community honestly and earnestly, we find that "there's plenty more where this comes from," and our cup is filled and overflowing. Sadly, this flow of grace can be overlooked, misunderstood, or misdirected by local politics, power plays, and theological scrimmages. When this happens, the flow of God's spirit is diminished, and all of us suffer.

The key, it seems to me, is to be mindful that we are standing on the shores of an ocean of grace, and to welcome and embrace the unimaginable flow of God's spirit that will fill our lives to overflowing. We simply can't hold it all in, and why should we? We must overflow, too.

## We Must Overflow, Too

Our practice of faith has been driven to the private sector—privatized. Even though God's kingdom is a place of abundance, an abundance to be received and shared, our culture encourages us to turn inward. Many of us have private residences with an ornamental and largely usable front porch. Our decks and firepits are in the backyard. We have personal phones, gated neighborhoods, private transportation, and we order our gifts and groceries online. We go to college without leaving the house. Our social media provides an illusion of connection but serves to isolate us and overwhelm us in triviality with a Disneyland of smiles and pet photos. Teenagers report much less social drinking and sexual activity, but their suicide rate is on the increase. It seems that they are so engrossed with screen presence and the number of followers and likes that honest relationships are ignored and marginalized. The deeper meaning and purpose of authentic connections are lost.

Yet the overflow of God's grace in our lives demands a public response. In essence, we must overflow, too. However, in our culture, the measure of worth and importance is derived from affluence—our income. But the impact of our spiritual lives is determined by outflow—and overflow. It is one thing to have a full heart, but it is another thing altogether to have an overflowing cup. We can say, "My heart is full," all the while holding on to it tightly as if it were a personal, private possession. But having a heart that is full and overflowing proclaims and shares the many blessings that have come our way. This is an important distinction because we must serve from a constant overflow or our cups will soon empty. And with an empty cup, we become spiritual beggars—desperately looking for something, anything, to fill our cups and hearts again. We must serve from the overflow, too, letting what fills our hearts fill the hearts of others, and in doing so, we discover that our cups remain full, an embodied confirmation that "there's more where this comes from!"

## Keep It Going

How then do we keep the flow going? Let me suggest four ways for starters. First, check your spiritual cup or your heart or your spirit, whatever understanding seems most helpful to you. Is your cup full and overflowing, empty, or somewhere in between? For most of us, it is somewhere in between, and if it is, is the inflow more than the outflow? It is critical to understand your own condition and consistently practice those things that fill your spiritual cup. A nurse told me recently that if you don't take care of yourself, you can't take care of anyone else. I totally agree—the notion of selfless giving and service sounds so good, so Mother Teresa-like, but the fact of the matter is that we need a healthy self, a full and overflowing cup, if we are to have any staying power and lasting impact. It does not serve the kingdom for anyone to passionately jump in, ignore spiritual self-care, then burn out and disappear. It seems that grit and grace go hand in hand.

Second, tell others about the blessings that come your way. Share your joy, and don't be shy. It is not bragging about yourself, but about God's work in your life, about the overflow of grace you have experienced. It is important for others to hear that God is working in your life and to understand that their cups can be full and overflowing, too. In fact, it is a normal and natural way to experience God, the gracious host. We all need examples to emulate.

Third, as you think about your calendar, perhaps meeting with a friend for lunch or over coffee, think about a question or two that you could ask about the blessings that they have received or the way that God is working in their lives, or simply ask them to share their spiritual journey with you. Everyone has a story, and if given half a chance and an honest prompt, most will share with you. Questions carefully and prayerfully prepared in advance can lead to deep and honest conversations about things that matter. Such conversations serve as a way of letting God's grace flow and overflow.

Finally, rather than trying to improve your prayer life, let your entire life be a prayer. Let me explain. Many of us feel guilty about our prayer times. If asked, we say that we could do better, and we feel guilty that we don't. We try to get up a half-hour earlier each morning to "spend time with the Lord" but after a short while we find it painfully unsuccessful, even embarrassing. Why? First, the idea of an early morning prayer time is too short. Often, by the morning coffee break, we are fully into our day and the prayer time is forgotten. Second, it segments our day—time with God in the early morning, and then on with the rest of the day where God takes a back seat to the pressing work to be done. And third, our prayer time is usually comprised of 90 percent talking and 10 percent listening. Certainly, there is nothing wrong with talking to God, but I have come to believe that prayer is most formative when we listen rather than fill an allotted time with our own words.

What if we took the spiritual concept of the flow of grace seriously and made it the centerpiece of our entire day? Rather than trying to have a more effective prayer life, what if we made our life a prayer? What if we began each day by praying, "Speak Lord, for I am listening; as I go through my day, give me spiritual eyes to see and ears to hear where I can let your grace flow through me to others, and have the courage to respond humbly and honestly"? What if this *was* our daily life—a prayer to be sensitive to the flow of grace and the part we can play as we share the overflow? It would make our entire day sacred, everything we do, even filing papers, washing the dishes, leading a meeting, sharing a meal, or picking up some groceries for dinner—because God is present, and we can never fully understand the powerful impact of small acts of human kindness. In the end, it is all grace at work.

At the end of the day, our faith journey is not a performance, not reserved just for Sunday or an early morning prayer time. Rather, it is an honest, intentional commitment to love God and neighbor with everything we have, all the time, every day, sustained by a flow of grace, blessing after blessing. We join with the psalmist who exclaims, "My cup runs over" (23:5), and say, "Me, too!"

## Scripture

Elijah was a prophet and miracle worker who lived in the northern kingdom of Israel during the reign of King Ahab (ninth century BC). At times, he was a person of great moral courage and faith, challenging the false prophets and defeating them soundly, and in the next moment he was scared to death, running for his life, and begging God to put him out of his misery. In many ways, I guess that he was a lot like you and me.

I want to focus on two events in Elijah's life that have something to say to us about the flow of God's grace. As it turns out, they were both mountaintop experiences.

## Mt. Carmel (1 Kings 18)

On Mt. Carmel, Elijah challenged 450 prophets of Baal to a fire-starting contest to prove whose god was true and powerful, and it was to be conducted without matches. This, of course, put the prophets of Baal at a great disadvantage, and Baal failed them miserably. They could not coax their deity to set their sacrifice on fire, despite all their desperate prayers, wild dances, and even painful self-mutilations. It was all in vain.

Then it was Elijah's turn at fire making, but before he started, he made his task even more difficult than it already was by asking the locals to bring water and pour it on the sacrifice and all around the altar. And they did—not once, not twice, but three times! And remember, this was done at great sacrifice because they were in the middle of a terrible drought and water was an extremely valuable commodity, so sharing was a tangible act of faith—and potentially life-threatening, too. The fire did fall from heaven, and it not only lit the wood on fire, but it consumed the sacrifice, the stones, even the soil. It must have been quite a spectacle. Remember, however, that now even the last precious stores of water had boiled away, too, and that made what happened next an amazing blessing. It started to rain. The people came with their last pots of water and went home with full pots, totally drenched, and their fields, vineyards, and orchards drenched, too! Their cups were literally overflowing as God demonstrated, "There is plenty more where this comes from."

## Mount Horeb (1 Kings 19)

You might think that such a spiritual display of heavenly power on Mount Carmel would be indelibly etched in Elijah's mind, but as soon as Jezebel heard what happened to her priests and threatened Elijah's life, he fled in terror and prayed that he might die. It seems that memory was not his strong suit. Elijah was instructed to meet with God on Mount Horeb. In that meeting, God reminded him that there was still plenty of work for his prophet to do, including anointing two new kings and his own successor. That Elijah did faithfully.

When we consider the movement or flow of God's Spirit, how Elijah met with God is instructive (19:11-13). He was told to go out and stand on the mountaintop because God was about to pass by and would speak to him. First, there was a strong wind that tore everything apart and shattered the rocks, but the Lord was not in the wind. Next came a powerful earthquake and then a great fire, but God was not to be found there. Finally, Elijah heard from God—in a gentle whisper.

How often have we looked for God, expecting (or at least hoping for) powerful and dramatic events, when what was required was to quiet our spirits and listen for the still, small voice, the gentle flow that fills and overflows our cups? Blessings come in many shapes and sizes, of course, but I have found that most are not accompanied with a laser light show. It is in the still, quiet moments, in the tiny steps of faith and in unseen acts of service, that hope and healing come, that we see blessing upon blessing, grace upon grace, flowing to us and through us into the lives of others.

## Some Practical Advice

Before we close this meditation on the flow and overflow of God's grace, let me offer just a few words of practical advice. What can we do to demonstrate that "there's plenty more where this comes from" in our lives?

Are there spiritual practices that exemplify and fortify this message? Thankfully, there are.

## Count Your Blessings

An old song comes quickly to mind: "Count your blessings, name them one by one. Count your blessings, see what God has done." Of course, there is a good deal of loose theology in many of the familiar choruses we learned in Sunday school, but I think there is great wisdom in this one. Count and name your blessings, see what God has done. We like Elijah often fail to remember what God has done for us and through us, so be intentional. Set aside some quiet time to remember and be thankful. Start with mindfulness. Make a list and put it where you'll see it every day. We all need daily reminders.

## Share Your Blessings

Don't keep the work that God has done and is doing in your life a secret. Go public. Share with anyone who will listen. The more we share with each other, the easier it is to do. And celebrate others' blessings, too. I have come to believe that our faith journeys are communal acts, not lonely pilgrimages. The more we share with each other, the more the flow of God's grace becomes real and unmistakable. When our cups run over, others can share in the overflow.

## Listen for God's Gentle Whisper

Start each day by asking God to give you eyes to see opportunities for service, to love your neighbors, and ears to hear cries for help, regardless of how carefully or coarsely such cries are made or the circumstances from which they emanate. Often cries of desperation are offered quietly, so it takes spiritual sensitivity to hear them and recognize them for what they truly are.

And along with spiritual eyes to see and ears to hear, ask for wisdom and courage to discern when and how to intervene, when to step back and let others take the lead, or when to let the situation run its course. We can all play a significant role in addressing the needs we see around us, but we are not called to perform the entire play by ourselves. Effective compassion is rarely a solo act. As a mentor loved to say, "We really do need each other." We honestly do.

Sometimes, others are uniquely qualified or better positioned to assist someone in need, and sometimes we have to step back and let things run their course, regardless of how helpless or guilty it makes us feel at the time. I think it is helpful to be reminded that we are the branches, not the vine. There are two pieces of good news here: there is a God, and it is not us. We are called to be a faithful presence in our neighborhoods, not to be the savior of the world. That role has already been assigned.

## Serve from the Overflow

Finally, we won't be able to care for others for long if we don't care for ourselves. Make a list of what fills your spiritual cup, and then work consistently to check off the list—more than once. For me, it is a ride in the country or a walk by the ocean or in the redwood groves. These activities are life-giving. They restore my soul and fill my cup, allowing me to serve from the overflow. God's grace flows through me to others, and my cup remains full.

Most cars have a sensor that signals when your tires need air. We either pull over and fill the tires or we risk serious damage and personal injury. This may sound silly, but I deeply believe that we need to have a sensor that signals when our spiritual cups begin to approach empty, and we need to be mindful of what fills our cups and practice that faithfully. And it is important to remember that we do not serve from a full cup, as good as that sounds, but from the overflow, demonstrating that there is an ocean of grace available to us—blessing upon blessing. We stand as witnesses that "there's plenty more where this comes from." Thanks be to God. There is and always will be. Count on it.

## Conclusion

In this meditation, we began by looking at the actions of the gracious host, who fills our cup until it runs over, signifying that "there's plenty more where this comes from." It is a beautiful metaphor for God's ever-flowing grace to us—blessing after blessing. After reading a story about the retirement celebration for Snapper, which turned out to be one unexpected blessing after another, we looked at the flow of God's grace in our lives and noted that while there is an ocean of grace available to us, we often approach it with a small bottle instead of a bucket—or two.

We noted the wisdom in the epigraph that faith must overflow, that it cannot be lived privately, and listed several ways that grace can overflow from our lives and into the lives of others. In particular, we suggested that instead of trying to improve our prayer lives (which is the cause of much failure and guilt), it made better sense to live a life of prayer, making everything we do sacred.

Two mountaintop experiences of the prophet Elijah were shared—one showing how what we think is an extreme sacrifice can end up being an unexpected and overwhelming blessing, and the other showing that God comes to us more often in a gentle whisper rather than in the windstorms, earthquakes, or raging fires of life. It behooves each of us to be mindful of how God speaks to us, and to be prepared to act when we are moved to do so. We were also cautioned that we can't care for others for long if we don't care for ourselves, too. Self-care is essential.

Finally, several words of practical advice were shared: count your blessings and share them, listen for God's still small voice, and serve from the overflow in your life. At the end of the day, we have an ocean of grace available to us, and it is a blessing to share that grace by serving and loving others. The gracious host welcomes each of us as an honored guest, and we enjoy a feast given in our honor. As we invite others to the table, they soon experience that "there's more where this comes from," too. It is grace upon grace, blessing after blessing!

## Questions for Reflection and Discussion:

1. Can you think of a time when you came to God with a tiny cup and received an ocean of grace, a time of blessing after blessing?
2. How might you share that time (mentioned above) with someone who is struggling with the goodness and generosity of the gracious host?
3. If you made a list of your many blessings, what would be the top three? If it involves someone, might you tell them? That, in and of itself, could be a blessing to them.
4. Has there been a time when you looked for God's blessing to come in a mighty way, perhaps as a promotion or a healing or some

recognition, only to hear God's gentle whisper instead? Can you share?

5. If you were to take seriously the idea of making your life a prayer, what would be "next steps" for you? Does it help to think that all of life, even the most mundane activities, is sacred and open to the grace of God? How so?

## Psalm 23

The Lord is my shepherd; I shall not want.

He makes me lie down in green pastures; He leads me beside still waters.

He restores my soul; He leads me in paths of righteousness for His name's sake.

Even though I walk through the valley of the shadow of death, I will fear no evil;

For you are with me; Your rod and your staff, they comfort me.

You prepare a table before me in the presence of my enemies;

You anoint my head with oil; my cup runs over. . . .

## CHAPTER 14

## *Surely Goodness and Mercy Shall Follow Me All the Days of My Life—Grace*

> Heaven have mercy on us all—Presbyterians and Pagans alike—for we are all somehow dreadfully cracked about the head, and sadly need mending.
>
> —HERMAN MELVILLE

### Introduction

In this chapter, we will examine the writer's summation found in the first half of the sixth and final verse in this remarkably short but powerful psalm. After offering such metaphors as the good shepherd, the gentle guide, and the gracious host, not to mention still waters, green pastures, paths of righteousness, tables set for us in the presence of our enemies, heads anointed with oil, and overflowing cups, something bubbles up from deep within the writer, who exclaims, "Surely goodness and mercy will follow me all the days of my life!" What a marvelous acclamation, full of assurance, praise, and thanksgiving. We will reflect together on this exclamation of praise, and then turn our attention to the meaning of finding and getting home in chapter 15. Then, as a way of a conclusion, I will share some closing comments about the three deep spiritual invitations that give energy and meaning to our spiritual journeys.

We begin this chapter with a childhood remembrance of goodness and mercy—grace at work in a small town in Michigan.

## French Fries of Grace[1]

In my hometown, Bernie Smith was a rich man—or at least we thought so. Not only did he manage the local grocery store, he also owned a small restaurant across the street—one with a neon sign over the entrance that blinked EAT in big orange letters. The chairs in the restaurant were covered with a bright red plastic, and there were four white plastic-covered stools at the counter. Bernie Smith was not only the owner; he was also the fry cook. We admired a person who could hold down several jobs at the same time.

Sometimes my grandfather would take one or two of his grandsons to Bernie's, and we would sit at the counter and enthusiastically consume a hamburger and down a chocolate malt. All of a sudden, a frozen French fry would come flying from the kitchen and hit one of us right in the forehead. What an honor it was to be the one singled out for such attention.

My mother shopped at the grocery store every Saturday morning, and once each month it was my turn to go with her. My three brothers had to stay home with Dad, so it was a real treat to be with Mom and have her undivided attention. My dad's attention was not something any of us wanted to pursue. If we didn't need to purchase a large sack of flour, I would ride on the bottom rack of the grocery cart. Sometimes I would reach out from under the cart and grab someone's ankle in passing. I thought it was kind of funny to hear a middle-aged person yell in that sleepy little grocery store. However, mother didn't seem to see the humor in such events, so I agreed under threat of being left home with Dad that I would refrain from any further such activities. It was probably a very wise decision.

One day while the cart was in the checkout line, I looked over from my favorite riding position under the cart and saw a big box of Black Jack gum on the bottom shelf. Given cover by the groceries in the cart, I reached out, took a pack of gum, and stuffed it in my pocket. On the way home, I opened the pack and started to chew. My mother noticed what I was doing, and without saying a word pulled the car over to the side of the road and turned off the engine. I was busted and I knew it, so I confessed. She told me that I would be summarily punished and then uttered those seven words that we feared most: just wait until your dad gets home.

---

1. First published in my *Morning Resolve: To Live a Simple, Sincere, and Serene Life* (Eugene, OR: Cascade, 2015).

I was on my best behavior the rest of the day—giving compliments to Mom about her hair (that wasn't easy), offering to set the table for dinner, and being as nice as humanly possible to my younger brothers. I even asked to be excused from the table without dessert and raced to my room. Of course, in the end, it didn't help. After dinner, Dad came to my room and made me cry by saying that he was disappointed in me. Then, he made me cry by administering corporal punishment (or applying some "medicine," as he called it). He said it hurt him more than it hurt me, but I failed to follow the logic. Anyway, I took my lumps and was ready to move on—but then the other shoe dropped!

I was informed that I would have to go back to the store, tell Bernie Smith what I had done, say that I was sorry, and pay for the gum with my own money. It proved to be the hardest thing I had ever done. Even though Bernie Smith was very kind about the whole matter and didn't turn me over to the police, I was deeply embarrassed because now he knew about my crime and that I was inclined to give in to evil desires of one kind or another. I seriously considered moving to another town to get a fresh start, but since I was only ten, the job market proved to be remarkably tight. So, I did my time.

I avoided the restaurant and the grocery store as best I could, but finally my grandfather talked me into having a chocolate malt with him. While I was sitting at the counter, a frozen French fry came flying from the kitchen and hit me square in the forehead. Right then and there, I knew that I had been restored to the community. You don't forget moments like that. It was a French fry of grace!

I learned a great deal growing up in that sleepy little town—mostly from experience, things that shaped and formed me. I learned that small things matter. I learned about right and wrong. I learned that I was accountable for my actions, and I learned that there were costs associated with making things right. But I also learned from people like Bernie Smith that goodness and mercy abound, and that these are some of the most precious gifts that one can ever receive—or give.

And I learned that we are shaped by our failures as well as by our victories—maybe more so. It seems that God is particularly active in those times that we come up short or fail or fall, yet resolve to get back up and make things right and try again. It is in those times that we are shaped. We begin to put down deep spiritual roots, roots that can sustain us during the dry seasons and nourish us as we resolve to live a simple, sincere, serene life—one that honors God and reflects the spirit of Christ in all we do.

Sometimes I imagine Adam and Eve looking over a green hedge back into the garden of Eden. How ashamed and embarrassed they must have felt—having been caught in a lie and being evicted from the garden. They must have wondered if God would ever speak to them again. Of course, that's our story, too, isn't it? All of a sudden, without warning, two frozen French fries come flying over the hedge and hits them squarely in the foreheads. It was a moment that they would never forget. How good it must have been to know—to really know—that they would not be alone in this world. God was still with them, and he still loved them dearly.

I think that King David must have felt much the same way when he wrote, "Blessed is the one whose transgressions are forgiven, whose sins are covered. Blessed is the one whose sin the Lord does not count against them" (Ps 32:1–2a). And after the whole Bathsheba affair, he should know.

And not only is our sin not counted against us, but God goes around making extravagant promises to us about our future and loving us dearly in the midst of our failures. I have a feeling that the first thing the father did when he saw his prodigal son's silhouette on the horizon was to go to the freezer and put a handful of French fries in his pocket before breaking into a full sprint. Perhaps the only thing in this world that is better than being hit by a French fry of grace is to have the opportunity every once in a while to throw one yourself.

## Goodness and Mercy

Let's be honest, we are all somehow dreadfully cracked about the head (and heart) and sadly in need of mending. There is very little dispute about that fact. As some put it, we are all cracked pots. Or as the Apostle Paul put it, "all have sinned and fall short of the glory of God" (Rom 3:23). Thankfully, we are not called to be perfect but to be faithful, and the good news for all of us is that "sin didn't, and doesn't, have a chance in competition with the aggressive forgiveness we call *grace*. When it's sin versus grace, grace wins hands down" (Rom 5:20, *The Message*). It's the story of goodness and mercy relentlessly following us, seeping into the darkest corners and cracks in our lives, places where we ourselves do not want to go, but when we do, we find that God is already there and at work. Thanks be to God!

During my doctoral program, I read a ton of books and picked up the habit of underlining passages in books that were particularly meaningful or insightful. Back in the day, there were no digital apps to help collect and store sources and citations. Actually, there weren't very many computer apps of any kind, so I would simply underline a passage and note the page number and subject in the back cover of the book for future reference. Fast forward to several years ago when I joined the faculty of a doctoral program in education. I started to critically read students' papers and dissertations, noting both insightful work and circling writing mistakes, mainly typos, spacing, and formatting errors. I found myself circling mistakes most of the time, irritated by the lack of detail and careful editing, and I would often lose sight of all the work that went into the paper, most of which was solid, insightful, and well-written. I became a circler, not an underliner.

I am convinced that since we are all in need of mending of some kind or another, there is much that we can see in others to circle, noting every mistake or failing or flaw, and it is easy to get into the habit of dishing out circle after circle. It is much harder to be an underliner, affirming that which is good, helpful, and hopeful, seeing the best in others—even in the midst of the cracks and wounds that are clearly evident. At the end of the day, we can be circlers or we can be underliners, but rarely can we be both. In a sense, we develop a dominant default, much like being right or left handed, and that's the way we see and evaluate others. The good news is that we get to choose our approach.

And we get to choose how we will see and evaluate ourselves, too. We often hear that someone is their own worst critic. Most of the time they are circlers, and their target of choice is themselves. In far too many cases, these circles become self-inflicted wounds. They are carried without any sense of hope or kindness, and they rarely heal. Even when we work at underlining others, we still circle all the little typos in our own lives. Imagine how demotivating, even devastating, it would be to receive a paper back from your professor, someone you admired and wanted to please, that was full of red circles and lacked any positive comments or praise—just circle after circle of criticism. Most of us would contemplate quitting and many of us would, feeling shameful and inadequate, unable to write a decent paper. Yet, we do this to ourselves all the time. When my last book was published, I found three writing mistakes—they were mine, not the editor's. My first response was to circle them, feeling like I had shamefully failed as a writer. My wife looked at me and asked, "How many words are in this book?" "About 85,000," I replied. "Well," she said with a smile, "do you think you might focus on the 84,997 good words instead of the three typos?" It was a valuable lesson for me. I can be a circler or an underliner. My choice.

And I fear that many of us approach our relationship with God in the same fashion, seeing God as the great circler—taking our life papers and returning them full of red circles without any praise or affirmation, and without much hope either. If that were the case, I would consider quitting the entire affair, too. However, the God that I have come to know is good, kind, gentle, loving, and gracious, not lurking in the shadows, waiting for the first mistake or crack that can be circled. No, the God that I have experienced *is* the good shepherd, the gentle guide, and the gracious host—the one who sets a table before me in the presence of my enemies, even when it is clear that my worst enemy is me. I have come to believe with all my heart that God is an underliner, not a circler.

## Surely Goodness and Mercy Shall Follow Me

*Surely* goodness and mercy shall follow me. What a bold statement. It isn't that goodness and mercy *might* follow me or *occasionally* follows me, or even *generally* follows me, but goodness and mercy *will* follow me—the writer is sure about that. Why?

Let me give at least two reasons for such confidence. The first is the writer's view of God. In so many ways, Psalm 23 flies in the face of what I call the Old Testament Bargain. It goes something like this: God is good, but God is judgmental, too, so those who are obedient are blessed with a plethora of good things (prosperity—military victories, bountiful harvests, growing herds of cattle, and lots of children) and those who fall short receive a plethora of bad things (punishment—droughts, floods, poor health, defeat in battle, and even captivity in a foreign land). The key, of course, is to please God or else.

Another view of God that gives me pause is that God is selective, that only a very few are chosen to enter the kingdom or have been gifted with some type of special religious knowledge. I call this the Special Club Idea. As it turns out, to be in the club there are usually a specific set of beliefs and behaviors required, and if you step out of line, then you are out. As a general rule, I caution against any religious group that draws the in-and-out line for the kingdom at its own front door and uses the back door to usher out anyone who dares to question the leadership.

Such views of God do not lead naturally to any confidence that goodness and mercy will surely follow us all the days of our lives, if at all. We would be more likely to exclaim that goodness and mercy shall follow us as long as we please a watchful, judgmental, demanding, and sometimes vengeful God, or we are selected for special treatment and inducted into the club. But I believe that Psalm 23 rejects the Old Testament Bargain and the Special Club views, instead inviting us to see God as good, gentle, and gracious, the one who invites us, all of us, to a banquet set before us in the presence of our enemies and celebrates us as honored guests. It is this view of God that gives us the confidence to proclaim that *surely* goodness and mercy will follow us. It is in God's nature to do so.

A second reason for being confident that goodness and mercy will follow us is God's own track record. In human resources training, I was told on several occasions that the best indicator of future performance is past performance. True, a person can change and sometimes deserves to be given a second chance, but overall I believe that this idea holds water. The same holds for financial performance. It is one reason that when we decide to trust our retirement savings with some company, we want to see a track record of solid and safe performance. No one I know wants to be told by their investment advisor, "Well, we win some and lose some. I'm never too sure that our approach will work. Easy come, easy go." Obviously, a track record matters.

So, what about God's track record? Interwoven throughout Scripture is the story of God's faithfulness in spite of one failure after another. We can think of Abraham, who took the matter of having a son into his own hands, yet God was faithful, and Isaac was born. We can think of Jacob, a real cheater, yet God kept his promises to him. And we can think of Moses, Jonah, Elijah, Ezekiel, Mary Magdalene, Peter, the woman at the well, James, John, the woman caught in adultery, and the prodigal son, to name just a few who came up short in one way or another, yet clearly goodness and mercy followed them.

And we can look back at our own experiences and see God's goodness and mercy at work in our own lives, often through the love and care of mentors, role models, and close friends. It is truly humbling to reflect on even our most difficult circumstances and see God's presence with us. Certainly, God's track record is good, and that allows us to look to the future with confidence, exclaiming, "Surely goodness and mercy shall follow me!" They always have—they always will. It is grace at work.

### All the Days of My Life

Before we end this meditation and draw some inspiration from Scripture, let me say just a word about the ending of this exclamation: "all the days of my life." *All* the days. This is important. In our instant culture promising things on-demand and same-day delivery, spiritual formation is truly countercultural. It is a process, a lifelong endeavor.

I grew up in a church tradition where the key events in one's spiritual life were to take a trip to the altar to be saved, and then a second trip to the altar to be sanctified. After that, we held on each week as best we could with the help of a mid-week prayer meeting to lift our spirits, bolster our resolve, and get us through to the next Sunday. As I look back, I can see that there was a great deal of time and effort spent getting each of us over the border into a new land (and on helping others to make the border crossing, too), but there was very little time spent on how to go deep, on how to make a spiritual home once we got there. The emphasis was on today, not on all the days of our lives.

I heard one of my mentors say that it is one thing to become a Christian, but another thing altogether to become a holy person. To be holy, I have found, is a lifelong spiritual quest, and careful attention to spiritual practices and disciplines helps keep our focus on the journey all the days of our lives as we strive to be shaped and formed in God's image—good, gentle, and gracious.

## Scripture

Over the years, I have had the opportunity to speak to a number of groups in a number of settings, and I usually end by threading together a series of observations and testimonies from the Old Testament: "His love endures forever" (Ps 136:1); "His compassions never fail" (Lam 3:22b); "They are new every morning; great is your faithfulness" (Lam 3:23); "As the mountains surround Jerusalem, so the LORD surrounds his people both now and forevermore" (Psalm 125:2).

In my way of thinking, it is another way of saying: *Surely* goodness and mercy shall follow me all the days of my life. Enough said. Amen.

## Some Practical Advice

There are words of practical advice salted throughout this chapter, so here I will only briefly mention four that will serve as a reminder to all of us who desire to respond in practice to the goodness and mercy that we have received.

### Shed the Perfection Expectation

As Melville points out, we are all sadly in need of mending. That is to say, no one is perfect, and I firmly believe that God calls us to be faithful, not perfect. That we can do. Yet so many of us are burdened by our own expectations of perfection and memories of our past failures, and we carry a deep sense of guilt and shame like a precious vase. Shedding this burden can be done with a firm decision to do so, but for most of us it takes the support of a few wise friends and mentors who walk with us and remind us that we are pursued by goodness and mercy—not anger, disappointment, and vengeful judgment. God's "yes" to us includes all our imperfections. Let's follow God's example and treat ourselves with grace and kindness.

### Focus on the Long Run

Rarely do we achieve spiritual insight and depth in an instant, like the Apostle Paul on the road to Damascus. Of course, even he was blinded and in a daze for a time and worked out his theology over a number of years and travels. That's why we speak often of our spiritual journeys, not spiritual events. For most of us, spiritual growth takes time and effort, embracing spiritual disciplines such as prayer, study, communion, centering, and service, to name just a few that over time shape and form us in godly ways. If you are unfamiliar with spiritual disciplines and practices, I would recommend that you seek the wisdom of a spiritual director or pastor. And you might ask, is there a best spiritual discipline and practice for me? Like physical exercise, it is any one that you will consistently do. Make it a lifelong habit.

### Embrace God's Track Record

We can look back across the ages and see example after example of God's goodness and mercy, often extended in the most difficult circumstances, and most of us can look back at how goodness and mercy have followed us, even pursued us, during particularly dark times. Given God's track record, we can lean into the future with confidence—count on it and keep walking.

### Underlines and French Fries

Make it an active prayer this week to be an underliner and avoid being a circler. Look for the best in others and be prepared to throw a French fry or two their way. Who knows, one might even come flying your way, too. There are so many aspects of life that are beyond our control and influence, but being kind, seeing the best in others, and extending grace is a choice we get to make. We are called to love our neighbors. This is a good way to start.

## Conclusion

As the Twenty-third Psalm draws to a close, the writer exclaims, "Surely goodness and mercy shall follow me all the days of my life" (Ps 23:6a). The writer should know. This is no thin, trite statement or an expression of fragile hope, but rather a testimony that swimming in deep water and drowning are not the same thing, to paraphrase James Baldwin. *Surely* goodness and mercy shall follow us. We know this because it always has. We can count on it and keep walking.

And it will follow us *all* the days of our lives. It is not a one-and-done proposition, but a lifelong partnership. That's good news, too, and it encourages us to employ spiritual practices that over time will shape and form us in God's image.

Some practical advice was offered to help us as we make our way home: shed the perfection expectation, focus on the long run, embrace God's track record, and be an underliner and throw a French fry or two along the way. At the end of the day, even though we are all somehow dreadfully cracked about the head and in need of mending, the good news is that our good, gentle, and gracious God is running to us with a pocket full of frozen French fries. It is an example worth emulating.

## Questions for Reflection and Discussion:

1. Why do we focus so much on our own failings rather than on our blessings?
2. Would you describe your default mode as a circler or an underliner? Explain.
3. How do you view God's default mode—underliner or a circler? What has shaped your view of God?
4. What disciplines or practices might you adopt to acknowledge that you are on a lifelong spiritual journey, not defined by a solitary event or two?
5. What story in your life best represents God's goodness and mercy to you? Why so? How might you share it with others?

## Psalm 23

The LORD is my shepherd; I shall not want.

He makes me lie down in green pastures; He leads me beside still waters.

He restores my soul; He leads me in paths of righteousness for His name's sake.

Even though I walk through the valley of the shadow of death, I will fear no evil;

For you are with me; Your rod and your staff, they comfort me.

You prepare a table before me in the presence of my enemies;

You anoint my head with oil; my cup runs over.

Surely goodness and mercy shall follow me all the days of my life . . .

## CHAPTER 15

## *And I Will Dwell in the House of the Lord Forever—Home*

> Maybe at the heart of all our travels is the dream of someday, somehow, getting Home.
>
> —FREDERICK BUECHNER

### Introduction

In several meditations in this book, you can find comments about going home or getting home before dark, and I meant these comments in both a literal and spiritual sense. In some way or another, we all are on a spiritual journey, whether we admit it or not, or know it or not. The destination is home. I readily admit that home can have a unique meaning for each of us since we have all experienced home in different ways, at different times, in different places, and with varying degrees of nurture and trauma. Still, I think that there is something universal about the desire to find and be at home in a spiritual sense, and I will try to unpack my thinking in this final meditation by first reflecting on my own physical and spiritual home experience, and then discussing what the verb "to dwell" communicates to me about the spiritual summons I believe we all hear and respond to in one way or another.

## Roots and Wings

If I were to choose a single word to bring back a flood of memories—mostly good—it would be *home*. I remember walking home from school after dark on cold, snowy, winter nights in Michigan, usually from basketball practice or a high school activity, and seeing the glow of warm, yellow lights from our living room and the porch reflecting on the snow. Mom or someone would be there to welcome me and offer a snack—if not a full meal. In fact, I cannot remember a time when I came home to an empty house or an empty cookie jar. As I look back, it was surely a blessing. For me, home was warm, safe, and welcoming.

Many of my memories of home involve meals, which we ate with great gusto and regularity. Growing up on a farm, my father was a 6 AM–noon–5:30 PM type of eater, but my mother insisted that we wait until all were home before sitting down to eat, and even though my dad protested, moaned, and groaned from time to time, Mother won out (as she usually did when she had her mind set on something). To resist was futile. As a compromise, however, if we were to wait beyond 7:00, a snack was offered to hold us over.

There was always plenty of food to pass around, and lots of stories and laughter as we recounted our day and reported on our exploits and frustrations, usually involving demanding coaches or misguided teachers who didn't understand that our entire lives did not revolve around the things they loved. As I look back, I see just how formative it was to share our meals together. We were home, and we were better for it. To this day, one of the things I enjoy most is to share a meal and have a good conversation with friends. Jesus broke bread with his disciples the last time they were all together. I am convinced that breaking bread together around the dinner table is just as sacred, and just as formative, too.

Another set of memories involves backyard events and activities. There were over a dozen elementary children on our block, and at one time or another, they all found their way to our back yard for sporting events, usually Olympic events (and sometimes even the entire decathlon) that were difficult to stage given the relatively small size of our backyard, even before it was dissected by a clothesline setup. We did, however, use the clothesline as the bar for pole vaulting if it was not laundry day. I remember repairing the clothesline on more than one occasion.

And we also had BBQs, picnics, and other celebrations in the backyard, usually accompanied with grilled chicken covered with my dad's favorite sauce. We also had an area for raising pets—ducks, chickens, rabbits, and geese at one time or another, and a big hole covered by a piece of plywood back behind the raspberry bushes. My brothers tell me that I dug the hole big enough for two so I could invite someone in and tell them a story. The admission charge was at first a nickel, then a penny, and when all the money had been extorted from the neighbor kids and my own brothers, I would give the coins back in order to start all over again. Honestly, I don't remember doing any of this, but it doesn't surprise me. I have always loved to tell stories to anyone who would listen, let alone be willing to pay for the privilege. Through all these activities, we learned to occupy ourselves, play with integrity, tell the truth, take care of each other, be kind, and have fun, too. These lessons have served me well throughout my professional career.

The third set of memories of home are bedtime memories. My older brother and I shared a small bedroom and slept in bunk beds to maximize floor space. At bedtime, mother would come in and sit on the lower bunk next to the dog, and our evening ritual would commence—a story, some discussion of a Bible story or church activity, a conversation about how we were doing and what we dreamed about doing, a prayer, and a reminder that she and Dad loved us very much, regardless of how we were doing—even if how we were doing was terrible. As I look back, I can see clearly that my philosophy of life, my theology, my sense of others, and my optimistic spirit were cultivated by my mother's love and wisdom at bedtime. It was honest, sacred business, teaching us to love both God and neighbor, and to see the best in others and in ourselves, too. She gave us roots and wings—deep roots with a sense of family and place, strong wings to fly on our own, and the good sense to follow the leading of the gentle guide. For that I am eternally grateful.

## To Dwell

I have said many times and in many ways that we, all of us, are on a spiritual pilgrimage or journey, and whether we know it or not, we are invited to undertake three spiritual pursuits along the way—to go deep, to be known, and to find home. And the older we get, the more urgent it is for this invitation to be acknowledged and pursued. When it is too late to go back and start all over again, the things that are important to us come to the fore. Some would say that it's both the blessing and curse of living into senior citizenship.

I do believe that we are invited to a more holy relationship with God: to go deep, to be authentic and whole; to be known, and to be at peace and find rest; and to find home. It is not entirely clear to me what the writer of Psalm 23 meant by the word *dwell,* but what comes to my mind are these three spiritual summonses—holiness, authenticity, and a sense of place. These are spiritual invitations to all of us, the paths we pilgrims are called to walk as we seek to dwell in the house of the Lord.

To be clear, going back home and finding home are two different things. We all come from somewhere, and in some way or another we have to come to terms with that time in our lives, but we are not called to go home in a literal sense. Finding home is a spiritual quest, coming to terms with who you are, where you've been, the relationships you wish to nurture, the kind of life you desire to live, and the kind of person you wish to become. Some of us have fond memories of the homeplace and would go home in an instant if we could, and some of us are still traumatized by that place, but all of us find ourselves on a spiritual journey to get home—to dwell with God, to be safe, to rest, and to be whole.

Long-distance hikers will tell you that returning home is one of the most difficult aspects of the experience because they have changed—their routine, their priorities, their insights, even their hopes and dreams, and it is hard to deal with others' expectations, especially from family members. I think the same holds true for those who return home for the summer after a year or two of college. Life presses on as before, but you don't quite fit in anymore. It can be difficult and sometimes painful, but it can also be an invitation to fly—new roots will come later.

In a spiritual sense, the same experience holds true. We have a desire to go home, but the pieces of the puzzle no longer fit. The established way of seeing God, worshiping God, and serving God may no longer be helpful or satisfying. In fact, they may seem tired, irritating, or simply irrelevant. It is important to remember that you have been on a long-distance spiritual journey; you are the one who has changed. There is no need to judge or make anyone else embrace your views. I think the way forward is to extend grace and kindness, and simply see your experience and growth as an invitation to fly—and over time, new roots will be established. The key, it seems to me, is to honor others for their investment in your spiritual formation (roots) but embrace and intentionally tend to your own spiritual growth (wings).

In so many ways, we walk together as we each make our own way home, all desiring to dwell in the House of the Lord. Our summons is to establish our own spiritual home, and support others with grace and kindness as they do the same. At the end of the day, we all draw on the care of the good shepherd, the devotion of the gracious host, and the direction of the gentle guide as we strive to answer the profound, God-given call to go deep, be known, and find home.

## Forever

It is difficult to know what is meant by the word *forever* in verse 6, but it is fair to say that what is meant at the very least is a very, very long time. We find the same word in Psalm 121:8, ". . . the LORD will watch over your coming and going both now and forevermore." Some translations use *forevermore*, and other translations prefer *forever*. I think the meaning is much the same. It is a long, long time—time without end.

And it is comforting to know that it is the Lord who will watch over our coming and our going, and particularly so since it seems that we are always coming or going somewhere, even when we don't know where we are going or what we will do when we get there. The Lord never stops watching over us. In my way of thinking, dwelling forever suggests a certain permanence, a place of rest and peace where we will not have to worry about getting home before dark because we are already there.

## Scripture

When I think about heading home, several Bible figures come quickly to mind. I think of Abraham, who "when called to go to a place he would later receive as his inheritance, obeyed and went, even though he did not know where he was going," and when he got there, "he made his home in the promised land like a stranger in a foreign country" (Heb 11:8–9). Many of us can identify with Abraham's journey.

I think of Abraham's twin grandsons, Esau and Jacob. Esau headed for home after a long hunting trip, so hungry that he was willing to give up his birthright for a hot bowl of soup—and he did. And Jacob not only talked Esau out of his birthright, but he also tricked his father, Isaac, into giving him the family blessing that rightfully belonged to his older brother. This led to a speedy departure from home and a long-desired return that worked out better than Jacob could ever have imagined. Home hadn't changed much, but he surely had. Wrestling with God has a way of doing that to you (Gen 25–33). Many of us can identify with Jacob's journey home, too.

I think of the disciples—Peter, James, and John. After his resurrection, Jesus came to them in their hiding place, but what were they to do next? They couldn't hide there forever, so they went home and did what they knew to do. They went fishing. And Jesus met them on the shore, made them breakfast, blessed them, and sent them on yet another journey. As it turned out, they had bigger fish to fry.

And finally, I think of Jesus, who having left his home after thirty years to pursue a three-year mission that would ultimately call him back to his first home, told his disciples, "And if I go and prepare a place for you, I will come back and take you to be with me that you also may be where I am" (John 14:3). And he could have said that they will dwell with him in the house of the Lord forever, which in many respects, means much the same thing.

## Some Practical Advice

According to the epigraph at the beginning of this chapter, maybe at the heart of all our travels is the dream of someday, somehow, getting home. I think that's right. Hopefully, these words of practical advice will be helpful to all of us as we make our spiritual journeys toward home.

### Don't Forget Where You Came From

My dad would always tell me to remember where I came from. Honestly, the older I get, the more this bit of family advice resonates with me. We all come from somewhere, and it is important to remember the lessons we've been taught, the values we affirm, and the memories we carry with us. For good or for ill, we have been shaped by our experiences of home. Even as we leave home behind in search of another, we take much with us. See your home experience for what it was and appreciate what you can. It certainly wasn't perfect—none are, but in most cases, with a little grace and kindness we can see that those around us did the best they could. Remember where you came from and make peace with it if you can.

## Dwell Where You Live

Home may be the place where you grew up, but it is also something that you take with you. You can make a home and put down roots even in the most transient of situations. Be mindful that wherever you live and whatever you do, how you live creates something of substance. Make wherever you live a dwelling place that gives hope, rest, and comfort. This is a sacred act, the seedbed where sustaining memories take root and grow.

## Learn to Fly

Whether we've traveled all over the world or put down roots close to home, we all need to learn to fly. By this I mean that we need to be cognizant of opportunities to develop spiritual wings, to be challenged, to grow and serve regardless of where we live. Much attention has been given to the necessity to put down roots, and I totally agree. Particularly in a time where mobility and flexibility seem to be the order of the day, roots are terribly important. But it is also critical to make the distinction between flying and just flittering around. When we fly, in a spiritual sense, we reach out with intention, stretch ourselves, and get out of our comfort zones in worship to God and service to others. It becomes a spiritual practice.

Prayerfully make note of ways that you can grow in your own neighborhood, church, or community. Ask for insight. What might God be calling or inviting you to do? Surprise someone—surprise yourself! Dwelling does not mean that you plant your feet firmly in the ground and never venture out, grow, or change. As you put down roots, don't neglect your own hopes and dreams or God's audacious invitations. Fly!

## Dwell in Your Own Home—Let Others Dwell in Theirs

When we think about dwelling in a spiritual sense, it is important to be comfortable with living in our own homes, not occupied with comparing our homes to others or trying to make ours just like all the others. We all are about the task of finding home, and it is ultimately a personal task. While it is certainly OK to look to mentors and models for guiding values, follow the gentle guide and live into your own heart. That path will surely take you home.

And it might go without saying, but I will say it anyway. It is certainly important to make our own spiritual homes and not try to live up to the dictates from any group or individual, however well-meaning they might be. It is also wise to grant others the freedom to construct their own spiritual homes, too, without insisting that their homes look exactly like ours or engaging in subtle forms of disapproval when they don't. Let the gentle guide do the heavy lifting. Our job is to be the lovers and encouragers, extending kindness and comfort to all as we, all of us, make our way home.

## Conclusion

I once worked with a university president who was fond of saying, "Let me tell you about this university *at its best.*" I like that phrase very much. Of course, the president and I knew full well that the university was not always at its best and perhaps never would be at its very best, but it represented an ideal, a hope, and a dream that the university would someday live up to its full potential, to its calling. I like to think of home *at its best*, too, even though we know that for each of us, our experience of home is different. But tucked away is an ideal, a hope, and a dream that someday home will live up to its potential, to its calling, and we all are on a pilgrimage to find that place whether we know it or not. At its best, home gives us both roots that provide stability and purpose, and wings that give us permission to go and become. And at its best, home extends a standing invitation to come back any time we can.

As we journey, I suggested in this chapter that we are on a spiritual mission, answering a lifelong invitation, if you will, to engage in three spiritual pursuits: to go deep, to be known, and to find home. And as we do, we begin to understand what it means to dwell, to be content and at peace, and we join with the psalmist who writes, "And I will dwell in the house of the LORD forever" (Ps 23:6b).

At the end of the day, we know that life takes us to many places. We often look back and wonder how in the world we ever got to where we are now. It certainly wasn't by our own wisdom or planning, yet regardless of how good it is right now, there is a spiritual yearning to find home, too. For some of us, it is a desire to go back home. For most of us, it is the desire to make a home where we are. For all of us, it is the desire to dwell in the presence of the good shepherd, the gentle guide, and the gracious host—forever.

## Questions for Reflection and Discussion:

1. What memories of home do you carry with you? How have you been shaped and what have you learned from your home experiences?
2. In what ways did your experiences at home give you roots and wings?
3. As you reflect on your childhood, are there things left undone, wounds that need to be dressed and addressed? What would be a good first step?
4. Of the three spiritual invitations—to go deep, to be known, and to find home—which is foremost at play in your life right now? Why so?
5. What does "to dwell" mean to you? How does it relate to your own spiritual journey to find home?

## Psalm 23

The Lord is my shepherd; I shall not want.

He makes me lie down in green pastures; He leads me beside still waters.

He restores my soul; He leads me in paths of righteousness for His name's sake.

Even though I walk through the valley of the shadow of death, I will fear no evil;

For you are with me; Your rod and your staff, they comfort me.

You prepare a table before me in the presence of my enemies;

You anoint my head with oil; my cup runs over.

Surely goodness and mercy shall follow me all the days of my life,

and I will dwell in the house of the Lord forever.

## *Closing Comments*
## The Good Shepherd, Gentle Guide, and Gracious Host

> Life takes you to unexpected places, love brings you home.
> —MELISSA MCCLONE

It is difficult to think of another six-verse passage in all of Scripture that is so familiar, so beloved, so packed with personal meaning for each of us, and so full of inviting metaphors that describe an authentic relationship with God. In 120 words, more or less—depending on the translation, we are invited to embrace and celebrate the work of the good shepherd, the gentle guide, and the gracious host in our lives. These metaphors are declared with a certainty that comes from trustworthy companionship, and a hope that follows from a loving experience with the Creator—not a God who spitefully judges and punishes on a whim or chooses a select few and disregards the rest, but rather one who offers rest and renewal, correction and guidance, and blessing after blessing to each of us as we journey toward home.

The *good shepherd* provides protection and direction as we make our way to green pastures and beside still waters. There we rest and find serenity. And we are encouraged to be mindful of God's care for us, and the need for our own self-care, too, particularly since God's desire is to renew and restore our souls, which is another way of saying our entire lives.

The *gentle guide* leads us along paths of righteousness for his name's sake, accompanying us as we walk through the darkest of valleys, even the valley of the shadow of death. As we journey, we are lovingly corrected by both rod and staff, offering courage and comfort. And we are guided by divine fence posts, guide posts, and lamp posts that point the way, whether we turn to the right or the left. The message to each of us is clear: Don't just stand there—walk!

The *gracious host* prepares a banquet table for us in the presence of our enemies, anointing our heads with oil as honored guests, and sets a cup before us filled to overflowing, signifying that "there's plenty more where this comes from." That's the way grace works. Indeed, we have found this to be true in our own journeys, so we join with the writer in affirming, *surely* goodness and mercy will follow me, and we know that it always has and always will.

Threaded throughout these fifteen meditations is my firm belief that we, all of us, are on a spiritual journey of one kind or another—even if we don't know where we are going. And as we travel, we are responding to a deep longing to go deeper in our relationship with God, to be known and loved for who we are and hope to be, and to find rest and peace in a spiritual homeland. And when the Twenty-third Psalm ends by proclaiming, "And I will dwell in the house of the Lord forever" (6), the writer is saying much the same thing.

At the end of the day, all of us know that words cannot fully express what or who God is. That is beyond human wisdom and skill. Ultimately, God must be experienced to be known. We know that. Yet, we do the best we can to offer metaphors that describe certain aspects of our relationship with God, and the good shepherd, the gentle guide, and gracious host in this psalm come as close to doing so as any I know. They offer praise to the God who loves us dearly, guides our travels, and graciously dwells with us as we journey to the place where we will dwell forever. Indeed, Love brings us Home.

# Psalm 23

The Lord is my shepherd; I shall not want.

He makes me lie down in green pastures; He leads me beside still waters.

He restores my soul; He leads me in paths of righteousness for His name's sake.

Even though I walk through the valley of the shadow of death, I will fear no evil;

For you are with me; Your rod and your staff, they comfort me.
You prepare a table before me in the presence of my enemies;
You anoint my head with oil; my cup runs over.
Surely goodness and mercy shall follow me all the days of my life,
And I will dwell in the house of the Lord forever.

*AMEN*

www.ingramcontent.com/pod-product-compliance
Lightning Source LLC
Chambersburg PA
CBHW031358230426
43670CB00006B/585